I0045799

HOW TO BE A MONEY MASTER MILLIONAIRE

101 Ways to Have More Money and Pay Less Tax

LINDA YAO

and

RAYMOND AARON

AuthoritiesPress

How To Be A Money Master Millionaire: 101 Ways to Have More Money and Pay Less Tax

www.AMoneyMasterMillionaire.com

Copyright © 2022 Linda Yao

Paperback ISBN: 978-1-77277-443-6

All rights reserved. No portion of this book may be reproduced mechanically, electronically, or by any other means, including photocopying, without permission of the publisher or author except in the case of brief quotations embodied in critical articles and reviews. It is illegal to copy this book, post it to a website, or distribute it by any other means without permission from the publisher or author.

References to internet websites (URLs) were accurate at the time of writing. Authors and the publishers are not responsible for URLs that may have expired or changed since the manuscript was prepared.

Limits of Liability and Disclaimer of Warranty
The author and publisher shall not be liable for your misuse of the enclosed material. This book is strictly for informational and educational purposes only.

Warning – Disclaimer
The purpose of this book is to educate and entertain. The author and/or publisher do not guarantee that anyone following these techniques, suggestions, tips, ideas, or strategies will become successful. The author and/or publisher shall have neither liability nor responsibility to anyone with respect to any loss or damage caused, or alleged to be caused, directly or indirectly by the information contained in this book.

Medical Disclaimer
The medical or health information in this book is provided as an information resource only, and is not to be used or relied on for any diagnostic or treatment purposes. This information is not intended to be patient education, does not create any patient-physician relationship, and should not be used as a substitute for professional diagnosis and treatment.

Publisher
10-10-10 Publishing
Markham, ON
Canada
Printed in Canada and the United States of America

DEDICATION

I dedicate this book to my mother, *Marie Y*. Thank you for helping me when I needed it the most. I am sincerely grateful. I love you.

And a special thank you to my sister and brother-in-law, *Celia and John A,* who are taking good care of our mother so that I may continue to pursue my passion.

I also dedicate this book to those who are opening it with curiosity, open-mindedness, and enthusiasm to understand a little more about how money works and become *A Money Master Millionaire* with a simplified approach by starting with a solid foundation.

And, of course, I dedicate this book to those who helped me in its concept and making.

IN LOVING MEMORY

My father, *Yun-Te Yao*
Thank you, Dad, for your sacrifice and the love you quietly bestowed on all your children. Although you didn't openly show your endearment for us, we could feel it—and still do even years after you are gone.

My father-in-law, *John Walker*
Thank you so much for your loving support. You were kind and knowledgeable, and your willingness to help everyone touched me deeply during the short years I knew you.

My dear aunt and uncle, *Betty and Winston Shen*
I could always count on you both to be there for me during my visits with you in Taiwan and Los Angeles. Your smiling faces and generosity are most memorable.

Al Cameron and his mother, Phyrne Parker
Thank you both for helping me at the North York Project Management Toastmasters Club. I sincerely appreciate your help.

Ruthe Simonsky
(one of the greats behind the Uncle Bobby TV show)
You helped me find my passion and purpose in life, and were a true entrepreneur to the end.

Mohan Kale
I truly thank you for your moral support and for continuing to work alongside me at World Financial Group (WFG) to the end.

Mark Andrew Tulhurst
You will forever live in my heart and I will always remember you for your passion for life, your curious spirit, and most of all your happy and sweet smile.

I love and miss you all.

CONTENTS

ACKNOWLEDGEMENTS

Family

First and foremost, I wish to thank my husband, *Douglas W,* for your endless support, patience, and love.

Thank you, Doris, for your support and your love. You are always cheerful and helpful, and you never impose yourself. I genuinely believe you are the best mother-in-law!

Thank you to my brother and sister-in-law, George and Kim Y and their children, Isaac and Esther; my nephew, Jason A and Abi and daughter, Inara A; Jacob and Shannon A; Jesse A; all the members of John A's family; Bruce and Nicole W and their children, Nathan, Matthew, and Ronan; my sister-in-law, Anne S; my brother-in-law, Rusty S and beautiful niece, Tessa; Debbie F and family; Rob and Sandra M and family; Bruce and Shelby M and family; my dearest aunt and uncle Hwong from Taiwan and their children and grandchildren; my mom's family and relatives from mainland China; my cousin Dr. L. Shen and her daughter, Dr. D. Shen; Li-ming S and her husband and their children; Li-Ching S and her husband and their children; John and Joy S and their lovely daughters.

Mentors

A special thank you to Raymond Aaron for selflessly providing guidance and mentorship for over a year. The one-on-one coaching and countless training sessions you gave me are priceless, and I will never forget you. I also appreciate your lovely wife, Karyn, who participated in the final push to get me going on this journey to entrepreneurship, and Danielle S and other support staff who kept me going on the right path.

I thank Joe Bauer for sharing your entire knowledge bank of promoting and closing techniques. I appreciate it immensely, and there is more yet to learn from you. I also thank Briana Bauer. You are an amazing person and a great assistant to your dad.

A big thank you to Loral Langemeier. With your help, I definitely can get my "7 by 71."

I thank Kane and Alessia Minkus for your coaching. Love your energy!

To Martin Rutte—thank you for introducing me to Project Heaven on Earth. It is so beautifully constructed and has given me more inspiration to forge ahead.

To Jeremiah at Advisorist and friends at Planswell—thank you for providing me with insights into social media for insurance agents. It will make all the difference.

Stephen Clarke, thank you for starting me on the road to entrepreneurship. I wish you all the success in your for-profit social enterprise.

Friends and Neighbours and their families

My thank you to Diana P; Sue H and Chris P and Son Shane; Erica S; Yoland M and Michael, Sharon S; Ajay and Indu P; Aradhana A; Shabbir S; Raj G; Lynda T and Bill M and children, Sean and Jill and their families;

Liza P; April M; Satie L and Benny; Karen P; Joan and Brent B and son, Fortius; friends at KPMG, Plexxus, Canadian Tire, Deloitte, and Apotex; Neil P; Sherry H; Sony Y; Willie L; Bruce P; Paul H; Meera K; Chiesa C; Kelly G; Yimei Z; Barbara D; Laurie O; Anne H; Cam S and Tracy D; Liam S; the entire Liao's family; Dr. M. Ortega; Dr. C. Tang; Dr. Chee L and Jenny C and their two beautiful daughters, Faith and Bethney; Mara O; David D; Diana and Alex M; friends from Spring de Spa; Annette B; Janet P; Amala P; Allen P; Andrea A.T; Nadia S; Elsie H and Richard L; Marlis and Martin B; Ping Ying (Grace) N; Abeba K and Dereje B and son; Ilkin G; Fowiz M; Wesley J; Ada L; Roger B and family; Shenglin X; Paul C and Li L and their lovely kids, Ethan and Snead; Tzu Hwa C and children, Luther and Louise and family; Louise T; Ally; Siewlay K; Monica G; Adam K and family; Grace H; Simon and Wendy L; Simon K and family; Catherine C and daughter, Lulu; Fernando B; Leo L; Farideh A; Alfredo R; Angela Y and lovely daughter; and friends from my childhood in Canada and in Taiwan; Yvon A; Donna R; Jesus F; Janet D; Heathcliff L; Faheem N; Bruce P; Sonny Y; Paul H; Simon C and family; Sarah C; Henry H; Friends from Spring Garden Church and The People's Church; Friends from Business as a Mission (BAM) from TPC.

Mentors and Friends at WFG

A special thank you to all my mentors at WFG: Rich and Cindy T; Monte and Lisa H; Tom D; Penny O and Ben; Connie C; Jonathan Y and Gina P; Alex H and Susan Z; and most of all, Laurie L and Brian C. You have shown me the way, and if it is going to be, it will be up to me. I am going to get it done!

I am ever grateful to Daphne W, who helped me and bailed me out hundreds of times.

I must also thank Yafu C and Chunmei Y; Garman L and Briana S; Joe W; Esther H; Jackie Y and Cheery; George C; Hanna B; Jingjing Z; Johnson L; Kurt and Angela Y; Rocky Y and Christine L and son, Landon; Edward Y; George C; John M; Johnny and Collette L and family; Mack C and Maria S; Annette B; Hanna B; Jennifer L and Gary T; Michael T and Kitty C and beautiful daughters, Belinda and Carina; Linda L; Margaret and William Z; Jacky and Cherry Y; Libby L and daughter, Aries; Sharon S; Andrea A; Xiaomin H; Simona and Dan N; Vincent L; Chester Z; Helen C and Kelly M; Mabel T; Tania and Peter F and their two handsome sons; Donald and Linda L; Gavin N and Olga D and two beautiful children; Micheal M and family; Stephen and Melaney T; Rosana M; Weidong Y and Ling P and their wonderful kids; Wesley J; Rebecca P; Ashley D; Hanna B; Sharon S; Jennifer L; Cindy G; Philip Z; Brandon L; Wilson W; Jerry T; Julie W; Dorine LT; Collette and Johnny L and family; John P and Alice Y; Alicia C; and Antonio I.

Friends at CPMP (Chinese Project Management Professional)

Special thanks to Tracy D, Paula Z, Kent L, Howard H, Robert C, Jie L, Jet W, Amy X, Charlie R, Joy Z, Cheng L, Phoebe W, Lixin W, Gavin L, Wei L, and Andy L.

Friends at CPA (Charter Professional Accountant)

Special thanks to Carol Anne G, Paul C, Lindy B, Ajay P, Archie O, Jerry P, Marlis B, Cameron S, and Emily Q.

Friends at NYPMTMC (North York Project Management Toastmasters Club)

Special thanks to Louise T, Grace H, June L, James W, Hilary F, Young-il Y, Nira S, Liza L, Sally P, Fatemeh S A, AhYoung L, Maria M D, Farideh A, Frank Y, Wendy W, Hin Lun L, Sally P, Jennifer C, Harman T, Helen G, Kenneth C, Maria M T D, and many, many other volunteers and club members.

I know there many other people who deserve to be on this list. Please know that you are just as important to me as those whose names appear here. Thank you for who you are and what you do.

FOREWORD

Linda Yao's *How to Be a Money Master Millionaire* is an honest look at her financial journey to becoming a millionaire. She tells you about her many investment failures, discussing the good and bad regarding each vehicle and relating how she finally turned the financial corner to independent wealth.

It's also a book about comprehensive financial planning, from someone who knows what she's talking about and has actually achieved the results using the tools she'll give you. Contrast this with the many financial advisors and planners who offer up paid advice but haven't achieved wealth themselves.

It is important to emulate those who've achieved the results you want. Well, here's a person who's done just that. She has become a money master millionaire and is willing to share her knowledge and secrets to successful financial management.

In Linda's book, you'll learn what money is and how to attract it. You'll learn how and where to invest. You'll also learn about cash flow, passive income, and taxation, to name a few essential topics. I highly recommend you read it and then contact Linda for some one-on-one coaching.

Loral Langemeier
The Millionaire Maker

INTRODUCTION

A Money Master Millionaire is someone who has managed to accumulate a million dollars because they have mastered the process of making and holding onto money. Your dream to achieve this level of financial mastery can become a reality easier than you think. Regardless of where you are financially, the place to begin this journey is with a few simple rules:

1. Pay yourself first

2. Protect yourself and your family

3. Educate yourself in personal finances

4. Invest wisely

   a) Discipline your saving and investment habits

   b) Don't speculate the market (use Dollar Cost Averaging)

   c) Diversify your investments

4. Find investments with fewer tax obligations

5. Do your retirement and estate planning as early as possible

I'll introduce you to these rules throughout the book. Take note of them, the steps as explained, and in no time, you'll be on your way to becoming a Money Master Millionaire.

CHAPTER 1

Why Start Saving and Investing Now?

"Don't save what is left after spending; spend what is left after saving."

—Warren Buffett

Nightly shelter use in the city of Toronto, Canada, averaged 7,000 individuals in 2020. The number is staggering and alarming. This was also the year of COVID, which resulted in massive job losses and business closures. Who knows what the long-term economic fallout will be? What's certain is that without emergency funds saved, many people who lost their jobs or businesses are in dire financial straights. Even if you dodged that bullet, you'll eventually face a serious emergency. That's a fact. So, it makes sense to start saving and invest your money now.

Then there's the high cost of borrowing for a car, a home, and your child's education. Saving in advance for some part of these expenses will reduce the drain on your pocketbook and improve your quality of life.

For example, a $35,000 car loan at 7% over 72 months will cost you about $8,000 in interest. Any portion of the car's price that you save in advance will positively impact your lifestyle.

And what about retirement? With the immense pressure being put on the Canada Pension Plan by aging baby boomers, you just can't count on the program being viable when you reach the age of 60 or 65. Besides, it only provides for bare subsistence; it's not going to give you the retirement of which most of us dream. Also, with the changing face of the business world, you can't expect a company pension like the one your parents or grandparents received. Therefore, it's essential—if not critical—that you save for your retirement.

As an example, my colleague's wife worked for Sears for over 30 years, and just before she was to retire, Sears closed. She lost her entire pension and had nothing else saved. I have another friend who worked at an airplane manufacturing company. His pension, worth $350,000 in 2000 and approximately $1,000,000 in today's dollars, is entirely based on company stock price, which sharply fell just before he retired. Don't misunderstand; having a company pension is a great thing, but it's also necessary to save outside of that plan. And for those who aren't accumulating a company pension, you must actively build up a nest egg for retirement.

Then there's the reality of longevity. People are living a good decade longer than they did 30 or 40 years ago. Are you willing to run out of money when you're 85 or 95? What will you do then? Sure, it's possible to go into a government-run retirement or nursing home, but do you know what that's like?

A few years ago, my sister and I were searching for a retirement home for my mom. She was 91. The government-run places weren't as nice as the private homes. The hallways were smelly and mouldy, and the showers were dated and often didn't work. I wouldn't want anyone to live in such conditions, let alone my mom.

Retirement homes are for elders who can still perform the five basic functions: dressing, showering, going to the washroom, eating, and walking. Nursing homes are for elders who can't do at least two of those five things. Even though she was 91, my mom could do all five, and wasn't allowed to apply.

Almost five years later, my mom is still in a retirement home (as she's still able to perform all five basic functions—albeit a little slower than before). Her room and board cost approximately $4,300 per month. She also requires between $500 and $800 per month for miscellaneous expenses. If she gets sick, we'll need to bring in nurses to help her, and that will be extra. Her pension and my dad's pension give her approximately $37,000 per year, which leaves her a couple of thousand dollars short each month. That means she'll continue to drain her savings.

Two couples in my mom's residence had to move out in recent years because they ran out of money. I don't know them; I just hear my mom talking about them. She was sad, but she was thankful she didn't have to worry about a similar fate because she knows that my sister and I would take good care of her.

I'm not telling you to be showy or a hero. Instead, I want you to know that children these days have a hard enough time surviving. It may not be possible for them to give you the financial assistance you'll need to keep going. What will you do? I suggest you start building your saving habits early and bit by bit. You'll be amazed at what you can accumulate if you start soon enough.

And guess what? Once you've built your nest egg, you can help the next generation and the generation after that. In fact, the rich look ahead two to three generations.

But what if you're in your 50s and 60s and haven't saved anything? Or what if you've lost much due to disasters? It's never too late to start again. Yes, it may be a little tougher, but you must have a plan.

I would seek a suitable financial planner, financial coach, or financial advisor and work with that person to develop your plan. And if you need to get a part-time job or another part-time career—so that you can catch up—I would do it now instead of later. Our time on earth seems short but much too long after retirement. Regrets won't help. What you should and could have done is in the past. What you can do going forward is all you can work with.

*   *   *

In 2009, author Simon Sinek gave a TED talk called "How Great Leaders Inspire Action." It was an 18 1/2 minute speech that called on business leaders to "Start With Why." *Why* isn't just a word: it's the driving force behind industry. And Sinek powerfully demonstrated that organizations guided by this concept would succeed more often than those that aren't.

Let's adopt the *why* movement here in this book. For example, the most important reason I save is that I want to have money to use as long as I live (my grandmother lived to 103, and my mother is now 95). That's my *why*. I want to rely on my own financial wealth. I don't have children, so if I ran out of money, I wouldn't have many people I could turn to for help. And even if I did have children, I wouldn't want to be a burden to them. Besides, it's totally false to assume that I won't need as much as I get older. On the contrary, I'll need more to have the same quality of life because I'll need to hire people to provide more services.

> Are you clear about why you need to save?
>
> If you haven't thought about it or are still unclear, you can go to my website at **www.AMoneyMasterMillionarie.com/TheBigWhy** for some assistance.

Once you've decided your big why(s), you're 50% of the way there. What's left are the things this book can offer you to make your dream come true—what you need to do and how to do it.

So, to begin the process, here's what I know: **Wealth is all about the money you hang onto.** The poor save what's left at the end of the month after paying all the bills. The rich save first and spend later, eliminating the problem of not having enough when they reach month's end. It's about what you save and properly invest right now. Not tomorrow or the next day, now!

I guarantee that if you don't develop a good saving habit now, you won't be able to hold onto money. The more money you earn, the more you'll spend, and in the end, you'll have very little to show for your efforts. After all, there are plenty of cases where people made millions of dollars during their lifetime but died broke (Billie Holliday, Mickie Rooney, and Judy Garland are famous examples).

On the other hand, I've had two divorces, suffered significant investment losses, entertained frivolous spending habits, and I still became a millionaire. Because I've learned it's about how much you keep rather than how much you make; I learned how to save.

Warren Buffett wasn't born with a silver spoon in his mouth. Today, he's the fourth richest man in the world, worth 70 billion dollars. A savvy saver and investor, Buffet has attributed much of his success to the excellent saving habits he learned from his father. Buffet started when he was six years old. "Save much and save early" is his number one Golden Rule.

In his book, The Power of Habit: Why We Do What We Do in Life and Business, Charles Duhigg wrote that 40% to 50% of our daily behaviours come from habit. So, if your actions around money aren't leading to you having more of it to invest, it's time to work on altering your habits.

> *Successful people are simply those with successful habits.*
> *–Brian Tracy*

You know, for most of my life, I followed my parents' philosophy that "money isn't everything." They taught me that my health, well-being, family, and friends are all more important than money. But while I recognize that's true to a certain extent, I believe money ranks as high as the air I breathe, the water I drink, and the food I eat. Without money, the quality of my life would be unbearably harsh. Just think of all those unemployed and homeless people mentioned at the beginning of this chapter. You can be sure they believe money is important. So, I've created a saving habit.

Now, I should let you know here that while I save money on an ongoing basis, I also spend a lot. For example, I saved some, then spent a portion of it on a car; saved some more and used a chunk to renovate a house; managed to put even more aside, then took a vacation; built up a significant emergency fund but had to spend it on an emergency. And I've continually set aside money for opportunities, which certainly have come along. At the end of the day, the key question is, "How much money do I have left in the bank?" After I buy the car, fix the house, deal with an emergency, take advantage of an opportunity, pick up more clothes, spend a little on jewelry and go on vacation—what portion of my savings remains? You must live and enjoy your life, but it doesn't mean you can't keep a portion of what you earn.

I'll repeat myself: the rich save first and then spend, while the poor spend and save what's left—which tends to be very little. The habit of the first defers gratification, while the other indulges in instant gratification. So, my advice is to save, grow your money fast, and then spend some of it. You're only young once, and what you save in your 20s and 30s can set up a comfortable retirement. Blow your chance to save, and you may be working for a very, very long time. And, all this being said, don't forget to enjoy living. Otherwise, what's the point?

CHAPTER 2

How Money Works – Traditional Teaching

Definition of Money

Money is a medium of exchange you and others use to settle, buy, and/or sell transactions. Its value is accepted within a governmental economy and internationally through the foreign exchange but isn't necessarily derived from the actual materials used to produce the coin or note. Money works because our society members are willing to agree to a displayed value and rely on it for future transactions. Money's primary function is to act as a generally recognized medium of exchange that people and global economies intend to hold and are willing to accept as payments for current or future transactions.

What is Personal Finance?

Personal finance is about meeting personal financial goals: managing your earnings, accumulating funds, and growing them. That involves budgeting, saving, and investing. It's about paying for things like food, clothing, medical, dental, mortgage, utilities, car, various insurances and taxes, as well as planning for schooling, retirement, and succession.

Think in terms of an entire industry that provides financial services and advice to virtually everyone you know. To come up with a plan to fulfill all the above-mentioned needs within your financial constraints requires that you become <u>financially literate</u>, so you can distinguish between good and bad advice and make smart decisions.

Traditional Financial Strategies

When creating a personal financial strategy, the first thing to do is set financial goals for yourself and your family in the following areas:

1. Create a Budget

Your budget is a plan you use to help you live within your means. It exists to help you save enough to meet your long-term goals. Unfortunately, most people have 50/25/25 spending habit: 50% of earnings goes toward expenses, 25% of earnings are directed to debt payment, and 25% of earnings are paid out in the form of income tax. There's no money left to save. Remember the lesson from Chapter One? Rich people save first, then spend. Poor people spend, then save the rest.

A good accountant can help you reduce your income tax and use those savings to help you pay down your debt. You'll then have money to save. With this in mind, the 50/30/20 budgeting is a better method that offers a great framework: 50% of your take-home (after tax) pay goes toward living essentials (rent, utilities, etc.), 30% is allocated to lifestyle expenses (clothes, taxes, etc.), and 20% goes towards the future (paying down debt, saving for retirement, etc.)

2. Create an Emergency Fund

It's important to "pay yourself first" to ensure money is set aside for unexpected expenses such as medical bills, a big car repair, rent if you get laid off, and more. More than 60% of working people don't have an emergency fund or don't have a large enough emergency fund. Traditionally you need to save three to six month's salary. After witnessing the effects of the 2020 COVID-19 pandemic, I would strongly suggest putting aside 12 months worth.

Remember, you can use a Tax Free Savings Account (TFSA) for your "rainy day" fund.

3. Limit Debt

A debt is something that's owed or due at the end of each month (in our society, this tends to be money, but it could be anything of agreed-upon value between the lender and the borrower).

Fail to pay off the debt, and the lender will typically charge some kind of interest. Debt allows you to leverage other people's money, but don't let it get out of hand. If you're using your credit card to support your expensive car lease and big house rental payment, you have a problem. It's known as "bad debt."

"Good debt" is still a liability, but it helps you build assets. For example, let's say you've bought a house using a mortgage. You'll have to pay back some of the loan principal every month, along with an interest charge. The hope is that the property will appreciate so that when you sell it, you'll be compensated for the interest and realize a tidy profit as well. The mortgage is a liability or debt, and you must make the mentioned payment to the lender every month. Fail to do so, and you'll lose your house to that lender.

In Canada, taking out a mortgage isn't always as good a deal as it might seem. For example, housing outside of Toronto and Vancouver generally isn't appreciating in the same proportion. My brother bought two houses and one townhouse in Edmonton, Alberta. Those houses haven't appreciated nearly as well as they would have if they were in Toronto. Yes, he collects rent money from each house to help pay the mortgage, but the appreciation of the investments just can't be compared to similar properties in Toronto and Vancouver. That means he'll have to hold onto the investments longer than he expected.

It's important to ensure you can pay your debts (good or bad) because failure to pay will result in some unfortunate consequences. You owe it to yourself to find out what those might be.

4. Use Credit Cards Wisely

Credit cards can be dangerous. But that doesn't mean they don't have their uses. Not only can they help to establish your credit rating, but they're also a great budgeting tool in that they're a great way to track your spending.

The best way to use credit cards is to pay off the balance every month or at least keep your balance below 30% of your total available credit. So, avoid maxing out credit cards, and always pay your bills on time. A guaranteed way to ruin your credit score is to pay bills late or miss payments consistently.

5. Monitor Your Credit Score

When attempting to build your credit score (something banks and other lending institutions use to determine their risk in loaning you money), credit cards are considered the primary vehicle. Some of the factors used to determine your credit score are how long you've had the card, your payment history, and how much of your available credit you're actually using (credit-to-debt ratio).

Credit scores vary between 250 and 850, depending on the reporting company.

250-300 = poor

301-350 = uncertain

361-500 = fair

501-700 = good

700-850 = excellent

There are a couple of simple things you can do to manage your credit score: have your bills come out of your account automatically and subscribe to TransUnion and Equifax (in Canada) so that you can regularly check your credit score. By monitoring your report, you'll be in a position to correct mistakes (and they do happen).

6. Consider Your Family

There was an older couple in Vancouver who had a beautiful home, bought and paid for. They didn't buy any house insurance because they felt they didn't need it. When a wildfire took their home, the couple lost almost everything— and they were left with temporarily worthless land.

It's essential to protect your estate assets and ensure your wishes are followed when you die. Be sure you make a will and, depending on your needs, set up one or more trusts for minors or beneficiaries not capable of handling money after you die.

You also need to look into insurance: <u>home</u>, auto, <u>life</u>, <u>disability</u>, critical illness, and <u>long-term care (LTC)</u>. Periodically review your policies to be certain they meet your family's needs through life's major milestones.

I've been asking people about what kind of insurance policies and coverage they have. So far, 100% of the people I've asked don't know and don't care. They know they have the various insurances mentioned, but they're too busy to study the policies. That's why a lot of people are disappointed when it comes time to make a claim: they think they've bought one thing, but they've actually bought something else.

Other critical documents include a <u>living will</u> for property and <u>healthcare, which is power of attorney (POA)</u>. I'll cover these topics in a later chapter. While these documents may not directly affect you now, they can save your family considerable time and expense should you fall ill or become otherwise incapacitated.

∗   ∗   ∗

My parents never taught me about money because it wasn't a subject ever discussed in their household. Don't get me wrong. They always provided for their three children. When there wasn't enough food, they didn't eat. So, while your children are young, take the time to teach them about the value of money and how to save, invest, and spend wisely.

7. Pay Off Student Loans

Student loans are often the only way students can afford higher education. How can you beat interest-free money from the government that's not repayable until you've finished your education? But you have no way of knowing what interest rates will be when you enter the workforce. If you end up with a high interest rate, paying off the principal as fast as possible is a good use of your money. But, if you're lucky enough to end up with a low-interest term with your bank, then making minimum payments and investing the difference can be a wise move. I've also discovered that some institutions will reduce your interest rate if you set up loan payments to come out of your account automatically. Ask your banker about available repayment options and pick the most advantageous to you.

8. Plan (and Save) for Retirement

When I was in my 20s, I was with a company that offered a pension plan. I didn't join because retirement was at least 40+ years away. I thought I had time, but time crept up on me. In a blink of an eye, I was in my 40s.

I started to save when I was in my 40s. I began to save even more when an insurance agent convinced me to buy a life insurance policy. The numbers looked good. And even though the numbers never matched what was on the illustration, he taught me the power of saving.

Today, I'm thankful this agent came into my life at a time when savings mattered. My husband disagreed, and he didn't purchase the same savings vehicle. We compared our retirement funds a few years back, and he had accumulated far less than I.

9. Maximize Tax Breaks

Due to our complex tax code, many individuals leave hundreds or even thousands of dollars sitting on the table every year. By maximizing your tax savings, you'll free up money that can be invested to reduce debts, increase your enjoyment of the present, and solidify your plans for the future.

You really should find a good tax accountant. He or she will be worth every penny. And, if you choose to do so, once shown the way, you can do your own taxes the following year. If you run into trouble, you can always revisit your professional accountant.

Years ago, my husband did our taxes. He thought it was smart that I claimed all my income while he submitted no income at all. Well, that turned out to be a huge mistake. I was an independent consultant, and we could have taken advantage of income distribution. By having an accountant revisit our situation, we were able to reduce our personal income tax rate by a few percentage points each and save thousands of dollars.

In another situation, a friend of mine passed away during COVID-19 and left many investment homes, mortgages, and hundreds of stock and bonds. Nobody knew what he'd been doing. I always wondered why it took him four to six months each year to prepare his taxes. Now I know.

Here's what I recommend: whether or not you hire an accountant, save all of your receipts, making sure to track these expenses with an eye to possible tax deductions and credits. A tax deduction reduces the amount of income you're taxed on, whereas a tax credit reduces the amount of tax you owe the government. Which is better? It turns out that a $1,000 tax credit will save you much more than a $1,000 deduction.

10. Reward Yourself

You don't need to deprive yourself because you're budgeting and planning. You can reward yourself now and then. Whether it's a vacation or an occasional night on the town, you need to enjoy the fruits of your labour. Doing so gives you a taste of the financial independence you're working so hard to achieve.

* * *

In the end, three key character traits can help you avoid countless mistakes in managing your personal finances: discipline, a sense of timing, and emotional detachment. Cultivate them. It's an effort for which you'll be rewarded.

Personal Finance Principles

Once you've established some fundamental procedures, you can start thinking about financial philosophy. The key to getting your finances on the right track isn't about learning a new set of skills. Instead, it's about understanding that the principles contributing to success in your business and career work just as well in personal money management. The three key principles are prioritization, assessment, and restraint.

Prioritization means that you're able to look at your finances, discern what keeps the money flowing in, and make sure you stay focused on those efforts.

Assessment is the key skill that keeps professionals from spreading themselves too thin. Ambitious individuals always have a list of ideas about other ways to hit it big, whether it's a side business or an investment idea. While there is a right time and place for taking a flyer, running your finances like a business means stepping back and assessing any new venture's potential costs and benefits.

Restraint is the final big-picture skill of successful business management that must be applied to personal finances. Time and time again, financial planners sit down with successful people who somehow manage to spend more than they make. Earning $100,000 per year won't do you much good if you spend $125,000 annually. Learn to restrain spending on non-wealth-building assets until after you've met your monthly savings or debt-reduction goals. It's crucial in building net worth.

Learn About Personal Finance

Since I became a financial literacy spokesperson, I've learned that few schools offer seminars in managing personal finances, which means there's a big gap between knowing what it is and how to do it properly. And there's so much stuff on the internet that you can get very confused. Who are you to believe? Well, I suggest you listen to those who have actually done whatever it is you desire to achieve. If you wish to accumulate wealth, I'm one of those people (I am, after all, a self-made millionaire).

CHAPTER 3

How Money Works – The Money Master Millionaire Approach

The information that follows is a new way of looking at personal finance. Now, it's not new in terms of the concept, but I've collected the information in a way that can help you understand why you should take the actions I suggest. You see, I believe that if you know the reason why you should act, your brain will find a way.

Where Families Need to Have Money

1. **Cash flow** – earn additional income and manage expenses.

   Consider this: If you find yourself having more month than money, you'll need to do at least one of two things: spend less or make more money. That's just simple mathematics. If you make a habit of not spending more than what you have, you'll accumulate money. You can also find a better paying job or a part-time job to subsidize what you need and achieve more money at the end of the month.

2. **Debt management** – consolidate and strive to eliminate debt.

   Debt management means consolidating all your high-interest debt (such as credit cards) and combining them with your mortgage debt. That way, the money you pay is reducing the principal. Also, you'll have only one payment per month instead of having multiple expenses, which is easier to manage and hence easier to pay down.

3. **Emergency fund** – save three to six months' income for unexpected expenses.

   It's important to have this, as we've seen during COVID-19. Many people are in financial distress right now. So much so that the government is providing relief money just to help them get by. It might be better to beef up your emergency fund to perhaps nine or 12 months worth of income. I know that may take you awhile, but in times of trouble some savings are better than no savings.

4. **Proper protection** – protect family assets against loss of income.

We all have car insurance because it's government regulation. We have mortgage insurance because the CMHC mandates us to have this—if we don't have enough of down payment. However, when it comes to life insurance, most people ignore the importance because it's not mandated. So, when something happens to the family's key earner, people end up in financial distress. Thankfully, today, there is also online application software such as crowdfunding to allow those in distress to raise funds from the community.

5. **Build wealth** – strive to outpace inflation and reduce taxes.

When your parents or grandparents put their money in GICs or bonds, the interest rates were high, and it was worthwhile. Now the interest rates have fallen below inflation, and it's not practical to put your hard-earned dollars in such vehicles because you're losing purchasing power each year. So, where can you put your money to make the most return with the least amount of risk? Keep reading, and you'll find a blended approach that I believe is the best solution. Just remember that each person and family is different. There's no one size fits all.

6. **Preserve wealth** – reduce taxation and build a family legacy.

The rich build legacies. I believe, even if you don't have millions, you can still leave a legacy to your children or charity. Money has four jobs as per *The Richest Man in Babylon*, and they are to spend, save, invest, and donate. So, once you've reached your potential, don't forget to donate and give back to society—like Warren Buffett or Bill Gates.

Financial Solutions

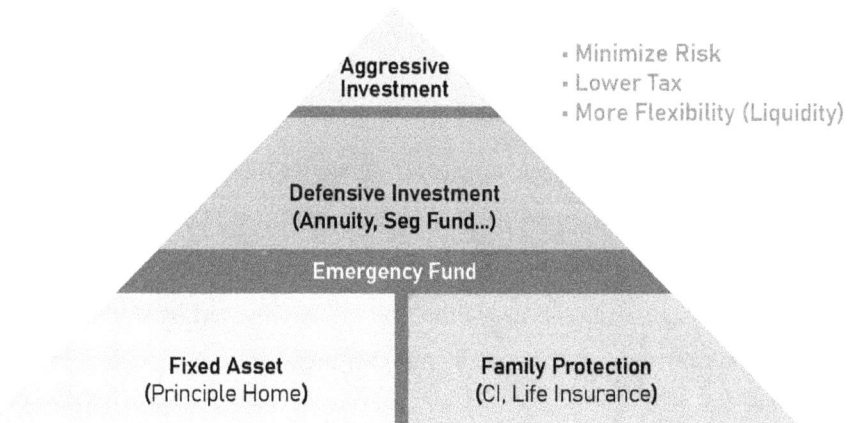

Figure 1

The key to becoming a successful money master millionaire is to have proper asset allocation from the beginning. You need to ensure you have a solid foundation before you jump to the next level. You can build little by little and not completely leave your current level until you're satisfied with the result.

Principal Home, Emergency Fund, and Protection

1. **Your Principal Home** – You need a place to call your own and, instead of renting, you may want to buy a home. It would be a starter home, so it might not need all the features you would like. However, the purchase will get you out of the rental market, building some equity. Don't buy something too far out of your reach. Also, consider a home with a basement you can rent out, which would reduce the stress of paying the mortgage each month.

2. **Start accumulating an emergency fund** – Save one month at a time. It may take several months, but keep going until you've saved enough to pay for three months worth of bills

3. **Protection** – Life insurance and health insurance are a must. Since you don't know what may happen in the future, you need to protect yourself and your family. That way, should the unthinkable happen, there's cash available. Crowdfunding can be done, but it won't be enough to replace your earnings for an extended period.

Note: With the COVID-19 situation, I suggest that once your insurance is in place, you continue working on your emergency fund until you have 12 months of expenses banked.

Level Two: Defensive Investment

A defensive investment is about putting your money where risk is minimal but the return is better than inflation. For example, if you're only putting your money under your pillow and it's not earning any interest, you're losing almost 3% per year because that's how much inflation is today (2020). But if you decide to put it in a GIC at 1.5%, you'll have to pay tax on the growth, so you're not much further ahead. Tax is like cancer; it eats quietly into your hard-earned savings. That's why I recommend a tax-deferred or no-tax investment vehicle. You can contact me at **AMoneyMasterMillionaire.com** for further information.

Level Three: Aggressive Investment

Once you have the previous levels established and you're in a comfortable financial position, you can aggressively invest a small portion of your money. If you lose this money, you're not going to worry that you won't have a bed to sleep in or food on the table.

Behind the Scene Theory

Where you are on the following x-curve chart will determine how you should invest. If you're young, you probably have more responsibilities (children, parents, and other family members) and haven't accumulated much wealth yet. As you get older and continue building wealth, you'll have more money to invest. Your responsibilities will also be less as your children become independent, your parents die, and other family members become more self-sufficient.

When you have more responsibilities than wealth, you need to protect your earning potential. Crowdfunding and websites of a similar nature are a new way of helping families in dire need. I think that's a good thing. But you need to recognize that such solutions represent one-time support, and even if the sponsors raised $250K, would that be enough to give your three kids the money they'll need until they become independent? I would say not. So, what's available? I'll touch on this in a later chapter, or you can visit **AMoneyMasterMillionaire.com** to get more information.

The X-Curve

This concept theorizes that a person's family responsibilities generally decrease and wealth generally increases over time.

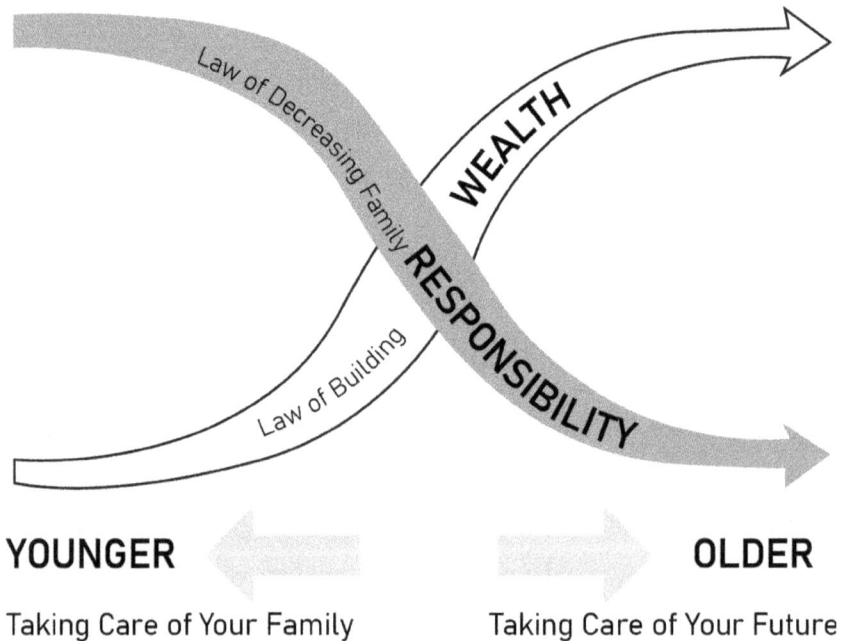

YOUNGER	OLDER
Taking Care of Your Family	Taking Care of Your Future

Figure 2

North America Household Wealth

Household Net Worth	% of Households
More Debt than Net Worth	10%
Less than $199k	56%
$20k to $499k	18%
$500k to $999k	8%
$1M to 19.99M	7%
$20M+	1% (Less)

Figure 3

Where do you see yourself on this chart?

From this chart, it's easy to see how 3% of the people control 97% of the world's wealth. Where are you now, and where do you want to be? Stephen Covey once said, "Whatever your mind can conceive and believe, it can achieve." Have a vision of where you want to be, and set your course. Ask the right questions, and your brain will get you there.

Can you see yourself giving up one latte and/or a chocolate bar a day? That's all it takes. When I first met my husband, he would go to Starbucks two to three times per day. At breakfast, he would get a large coffee with a muffin. For lunch, he would buy a coffee and a sandwich. Later on, for a snack, he would get a latte. At the time, this added up to between $20 and $25 per day. By reducing his purchases to just two cups of coffee each day, he saved thousands of dollars. Once in a while, he would splurge and buy the other stuff. Most of the time, though, he would make his lunch or take leftovers from our fridge.

Many articles on the internet will tell you that saving money isn't the way to go, that the better way is to invest properly and take calculated risks. I think you need to determine which approach is best for you. I would also pose the question, "How can you invest if you don't have any money?" Well, you can undoubtedly borrow it (as many people do at RRSP time), but that's taking on debt. The more debt you take on, the more money you'll need to service the debt. It's a vicious circle.

As a novice, you won't know what's right and what's wrong for you, so I suggest avoiding internet advice. By the time you try the proposed method, and it doesn't work, you've lost money. I specialize in helping people create wealth.

Contact me at **AMoneyMasterMillionaire.com**

To learn how to construct your personal financial strategy
from A through Z.

Time is Money

You hear a lot about this when you're working because your time is billable to clients. Well, what about your money in the sense of how it's invested? When I was working, I didn't care where I put my money. I just saved it in the bank and earned next to nothing in interest. My money only grew because I kept adding to it. I never looked at my rate of return or where I should invest.

Nevertheless, I continued to make money, and I saved more. Now that I've accumulated a sizeable chunk, I realize I must have made good returns somewhere. The problem is I have no idea what made me money. I can't replicate the occurrence.

If you start saving when you're 25, you only have to put away $655.30 per month at a 5% average return, and you'll have $1 million at age 65. That's just an example, and I'm not suggesting that you don't eat properly or provide for your family to save this amount. Use time to your advantage and save in proportions you can afford.

If retirement is 30 years away and you want to accumulate a million dollars, you'll need to put away $1,201.55 per month at a 5% rate of return. If you haven't started saving by the time you reach your 60s, you'll have to save $14,704.57 per month. How realistic is that?

The Cost of Waiting

Get time on your side

It's easy to put off saving for retirement for another day, but waiting can set you back more than you might imagine.

FOR EXAMPLE*

- To save $1 million for retirement over 40 years you need to put away $655.30 per month in an 5% tax-deferred account.
- If you have only five years, that monthly savings goal changes to $14,704.57.*

Make Time Your Friend. Start Saving Today!

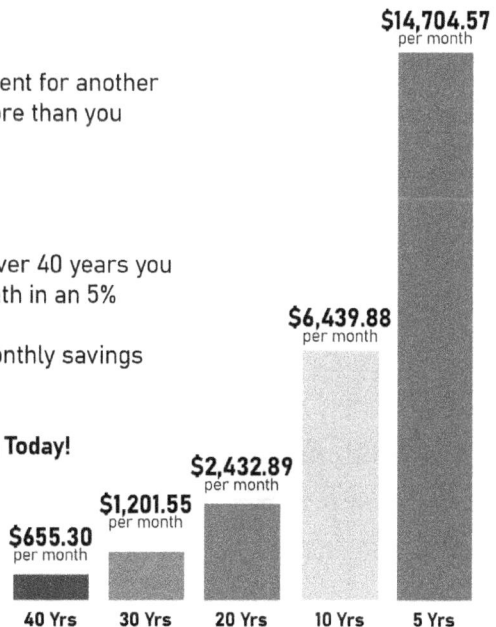

$655.30 per month — 40 Yrs
$1,201.55 per month — 30 Yrs
$2,432.89 per month — 20 Yrs
$6,439.88 per month — 10 Yrs
$14,704.57 per month — 5 Yrs

Figure 4

The first thing that jumped out at me from the preceding chart is that it's realistic for me.

I was a good saver, but I also spent a lot. In my 20s and 30s, I saved money but then I spent it (buying a car, renovating a house, going on vacations). In the end, I had very little to show for my effort. It wasn't until I was in my 40s that I accumulated money, saving over $2,000 per month. As a result, now that I'm in my 60s, I have a good-sized retirement fund.

The point here is that the chart will show you how much you need to save to have $1,000,000 at age 65, no matter what age you are. I believe you'll probably need at least $500K to retire comfortably in today's economy (with COVID-19 and expected inflation, you might even need more). Without it, you won't be able to retire, or you'll end up retiring with a limited budget.

A close friend of mine retired in her 40s, and she was very good with money. Even with that, inflation caused her to live within a strict budget. If that suits your lifestyle, I'd say it's fine. But if you're looking for luxurious living in your retirement, you'll need to save more now and put your money to work for you.

Compound interest is the eighth wonder of the world.
He who understands it earns it; he who doesn't, pays it.

–Albert Einstein

Warren Buffett is an American investor, business tycoon, philanthropist, and CEO of Berkshire Hathaway. He's probably the most successful investor in the world, having accumulated a net worth of over US $78.9 billion at the time of writing this book.

Buffett's authorized biography is titled *The Snowball*, referencing The Snowball Effect. It states, metaphorically, that a snowball starts from an initial state of small significance and builds upon itself, becoming larger and ever more powerful, gaining a kind of self-perpetuating momentum. You see, Buffett understands the magic of compounding, which allowed him to multiply his fortune by over 7,000 %.

Warren Buffett began rolling his snowball down the hill in his early teens and continues growing it today (he turned 90 in 2020), but it's the compounding of his wealth that separates him from the crowd. His ability to achieve a higher than average return than most, and the fact that he has compounded it for a long time, has produced astonishing results.

Sure, the level of wealth Buffett has accumulated would be hard to replicate, but you don't need tens of billions of dollars to achieve a comfortable lifestyle. The concept is quite simple, really, but it's not easy. The key lesson to learn is that today's beneficial actions will provide much greater benefits over time—due to compounding.

To illustrate the power of compound interest, let's compare Jennifer and Grant, who both invested money for eight consecutive years. Jennifer began investing $500 per month for retirement purposes when she turned 27, and she continued to do so until she was 35. Grant, on the other hand, decided to invest in his lifestyle. He was 57 before he recognized the need to save some money for retirement. Grant then began to put away $500 per month and did so until he was 65. So, both individuals directed $500 per month into investments for eight years, except Jennifer did it much earlier. Let's compare their results:

Age	Jennifer (3% Return)		Grant (3% Return)		Grant (3% Return)	
	Savings $500 * 12	Accumulated $	Savings	Accumulated $	Savings $1K * 12	Accumulated $
28	$6,000	$6,180.00				
29	$6,000	$12,545.40				
30	$6,000	$19,101.76				
31	$6,000	$25,854.81				
32	$6,000	$32,810.46				
33	$6,000	$39,974.77				
34	$6,000	$47,354.02				
35	$6,000	$54,954.64				
...						
57	0	$ 102,231.81	$ 6,000	$ 6,180.00	$12,000	$ 12,360.00
58	0	$ 105,298.77	$ 6,000	$ 12,545.40	$12,000	$ 25,090.80
59	0	$ 108,457.73	$ 6,000	$ 19,101.76	$12,000	$ 38,203.52
60	0	$ 111,711.46	$ 6,000	$ 25,854.81	$12,000	$ 51,709.63
61	0	$ 115,062.81	$ 6,000	$ 32,810.46	$12,000	$ 65,620.92
62	0	$ 118,514.69	$ 6,000	$ 39,974.77	$12,000	$ 79,949.55
63	0	$ 122,070.13	$ 6,000	$ 47,354.02	$12,000	$ 94,708.03
64	0	$ 125,732.23	$ 6,000	$ 54,954.64	$12,000	$ 109,909.27
65	$48,000	$ 129,504.20	$48,000	$ 56,603.28	$96,000	$ 113,206.55

Figure 5

The calculations above assume no inflation, which reflects the true purchasing power of accumulated capital. The difference here is spectacular! Jane's accumulated savings are more than twice what Grant managed to put away.

Rule of 72

The Rule of 72 is a way of estimating investment returns, taught by Albert Einstein. It refers to how interest can grow your investments when it's compounded, something he called the eighth wonder of the world. Warren Buffett adopted this rule, and so should you.

The Formula for the Rule of 72

Years for an investment to double = 72/Interest Rate

Where: Interest Rate = Rate of return on an investment

Taxable, Tax Deferred, and No Tax Investments

I love to see my money grow, and I love to have more money. In an earlier chapter, I mentioned that it's not about how much money you make but rather how much you keep. So, how do you keep more in your pocket if all you have are taxable and tax-deferred investments? Honestly? You can't do it because the government is eventually going to get its share.

For example, in taxable investments, you're saving after-tax money, but you're taxed on any gain you make. In a tax-deferred investment, you're saving and growing your money free of any taxation. However, anything you withdraw is taxed as income. That's terrific while you're young. After all, you're saving for retirement. And the gurus will tell you not to worry about eventual taxation because you'll be in a lower tax bracket when you retire, and pay less overall tax. The problem I have (and that many people have) is that my tax rate is much higher now than it was 30 years ago. I'm actually paying more tax than I would have if I had gone with a taxable investment. The other thing I didn't consider is that I must take out a specified amount from my registered investments when I reach 71. If I have too much RRSP money combined with the CPP and OAS, I won't qualify for the GIS. It's a real problem.

Canadian Retirement Vehicles

Registered Retirement Saving Plan (RRSP) – This is where you park your retirement savings when you're working.

Registered Retirement Income Fund (RRIF) – When you reach 71, the government wants you to take out money steadily, so you must convert all your RRSPs to a RRIF. Your bank can then withdraw taxable funds from this account at a minimum rate. If you fail to do this, the government will penalize you.

Canada Pension Plan (CPP) – If you work in Canada, you'll contribute to this plan, so you're entitled to get some money at retirement. Whether you receive the full monthly amount or not depends on the length of time you contribute and how much you contribute. This year the maximum CPP contribution is $1,175.83. You can find additional rules and regulations on the Canadian Government Website (https://www.canada.ca/).

Old Age Security (OAS) – Every Canadian resident gets this money. If you've lived here for more than 40 years (after age 18), you should receive the maximum monthly amount. Immigrants and permanent residents will need to reside in Canada for more than ten years to qualify for the OAS. You must also declare all your income—here and abroad. That's because if you make too much, the government will claw back the pension.

Guaranteed Income Supplement (GIS) – When you declare your CPP, the GIS indicator turns on. The Canadian government will automatically send you a monthly cheque as long your total income falls below a threshold. In 2020, this amount is $18,624 for single people and $24,576 for couples. See the Government of Canada website for more details.

Types of Investment Vehicles

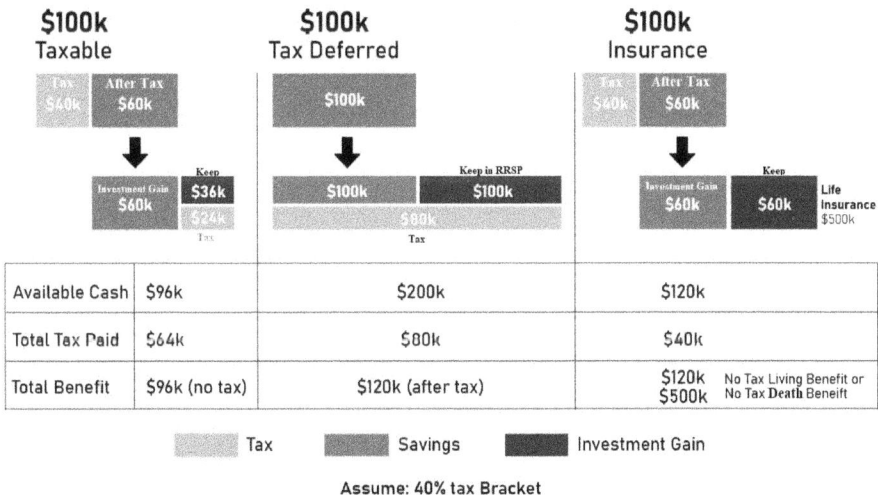

	$100k Taxable	$100k Tax Deferred	$100k Insurance
Available Cash	$96k	$200k	$120k
Total Tax Paid	$64k	$80k	$40k
Total Benefit	$96k (no tax)	$120k (after tax)	$120k No Tax Living Benefit or $500k No Tax Death Beneift

Tax   Savings   Investment Gain

Assume: 40% tax Bracket

Figure 6

Enough about the theory. Let's refer to the chart above and see what we can do with this information. As you get older, you'll want to move your money from the chart's left side to the right side. Why? If you have a lot of money in non-registered accounts, you're getting taxed on each year's growth. That will decrease your spending money. If you have a lot of money in your RRSPs or RRIF, you're getting taxed as you use that money. However, if you're using cash from a Tax Free Savings Account (TFSA) or money accumulated in life insurance, you're not taxed. That's the best place to be because you can use every dollar you take out, and you're not obligated to report it as income for tax purposes, which will allow you the opportunity to keep your income below the threshold and qualify for the GIS. I should point out this isn't a way to cheat the government; it's legitimate and intelligent planning retirement planning.

Contact me at **AMoneyMasterMillionaire.com** and schedule a preliminary appointment to show you the details.

CHAPTER 4
Cash Flow 101

What is Cash Flow?

Cash flow is the amount of money you bring in (personal, business, or investment income) minus the amount of money you spend. Ideally, the result should be positive. Let's say you make $1,000 and you spend $1,500. Your cash flow is negative $500.00. If you make $1,000 and spend $800, you would have a positive cash flow of $200.00. Always strive for a positive cash flow.

Earlier I wrote about having more month than money. All that means is that you've spent more money than you earned. If you consistently do this, you'll end up owing more and more money. You'll find yourself needing someone you trust to help you consolidate debt and start to pay it off. If not, sooner or later, you'll have to declare bankruptcy. There are many consequences when you declare bankruptcy. For example, it will ruin your credit rating for a long time, and it will be exceedingly difficult to borrow money. You need to get yourself out of debt!

It's estimated that the Canadian government will spend at least $400 billion by early 2021 because of the COVID-19 pandemic. This debt will need to be paid by its citizens through higher taxes. If the interest rate rises and the government can't pay back what it owes, there could be severe consequences.

> To learn more about bankruptcy and related issues, visit
> **http://www.cpacanada.ca/en/news/canada/2020-12-09-personal-bankruptcy**

How to Have More Positive Cash Flow

We're educated in our school system to study hard and get a JOB, which is sometimes defined as being "Just Over Broke." So, if you need more cash flow, you can do the following:

- **Get more education** to get a better JOB: a university Master's, PhD, or medical degree. It's the conventional way of thinking. But regardless of how much education you have, you still have an earnings ceiling because you're working for someone else, making their dream come true.

- **Start your own business**. In this instance, I don't want you to think about businesses that require your time in exchange for money. That's just buying a job. What I'm referring to here is the kind of business where you invest in employees who, in turn, create income for you—even when you're asleep.

But remember that, in most cases, starting your own business—like buying property for rent or a franchise—requires a lot of initial capital, and the risk associated with it is significant. Statistics reflect the fact that 97% of entrepreneurs will go broke at some point.

Canadian business statistics indicate that about 70 percent of new small businesses (less than 100 employees) survive for five years. What this means is that approximately 7,000 companies go bankrupt every year. The main reason for these business failures seems to be inexperienced management. That equates to poor planning. What a waste! Something as simple as constructing a solid business plan could eliminate most business failures. Another crucial task is to determine the cash flow you'll require to live and run your business; you can't assume it will generate enough income each month to pay all the bills.

- **Invest**. This is where you use your money to create more money—through investment in the stock or bond market, real estate, established or start-up businesses, etc. These are usually vehicles that return your capital along with a certain percentage of interest or earnings.

Why Do You Have to Save Money?

Some people are actually against saving. They believe their earnings potential as an employee or business owner is sufficient for their needs. But what happens if an injury occurs, a job is lost, the business goes under, or you retire? What then? You must have access to money when your cash flow dries up. That's why you save.

According to Wikipedia, Donald Trump has never filed for personal bankruptcy. Still, hotels and casino businesses of his have declared bankruptcy six times between 1991 and 2009 due to their inability to meet required payments and to re-negotiate debt with banks, owners of stock and bonds, and various small businesses (unsecured creditors). My point? Even the extremely rich need excellent cash flow and money in reserve.

2020 was a brutal year for retail businesses and restaurants. The COVID-19 restrictions and the shift in consumer habits dried up cash flow, resulting in massive debt, closures, and bankruptcies. For example, one report indicated that 17% of U.S. restaurants (about 110,000) permanently closed their doors this year, with thousands more in serious trouble. Such businesses typically run on tight margins, with no savings to fall back on. And what about all the employees who lost their jobs due to the closures? You can bet that most had little or no savings to fall back on.

Saving for Different Purposes

- **Retirement**

You can start to save for your retirement at any age. The earlier you start, the better off you'll be. Most entrepreneurs think they don't need to save and that when they hit big, they'll have all the money in the world for their retirement. If you look at the statistics, only 3% of entrepreneurs have millions of dollars. By the time you realize you're not in the top 3%, it will be too late. While an entrepreneur must be all in, he or she must still think carefully. Even entrepreneurs need food and shelter.

Many people use an RRSP to put away money for retirement. It's a long-term vehicle that allows you to defer taxes. Therefore, you shouldn't use the funds for emergency purposes.

In Canada, you can use part of your RRSP to purchase your first home (up to $35K for an individual and $70K if buying with your spouse or partner). That's great, but remember you have to put the funds back. Also, money removed from your RRSP no longer grows tax-free. You need to factor that in when you do your calculations.

As an employee, a good place to save is in your RRSP. If you earn more than $45K per annum, you should do that. An option I'd urge you to take a look at is company-sponsored RRSPs because if your employer matches contributions at 3% or 4%, it would be worth your while. It's like giving yourself a raise. And by taking out the RRSP at the company level, you aren't putting in after-tax money.

However, if you earn less than $45K, it might be better to save in a non-registered account (RRSPs don't provide as many benefits for lower-income earners). Just realize that when you save outside of your RRSP in a non-registered account, you'll have to pay tax as you buy and sell, which will slow down your savings growth.

One alternative is to invest in universal life, whole life, or whole life participating insurance. An insurance agent approached me when I was in my 40s, and I ended up buying many policies. That forced me to save, and today I appreciate that intervention. One of the best ways to save is to put the money where you can't easily get access to it and still have your savings grow at a reasonable rate (funds inside a life insurance policy grow tax-free).

- **TFSA / Emergency Fund**

A Tax Free Savings Account is a great way to save and get a good return without paying tax on investment growth. The money you put in a TFSA is after-tax money—unlike your RRSP, which is pre-tax money. Current tax law states that if you were over the age of 18 on January 1st, 2009, you could take advantage of this kind of savings vehicle.

If you've never opened a TFSA, you can contribute up to $69,500 today:

- $5,000 for each year from 2009 to 2012;

- $5,500 for each of 2013 and 2014;

- $10,000 for 2015;

- $5,500 for each of 2016, 2017 and 2018; and

- $6,000 for 2019 and 2020.

If you take out the money, it's tax-free. That makes your TFSA a better choice for an emergency fund than an RRSP.

Other things to know about your TFSA:

1. You can invest in just about anything. But be aware that while you don't pay tax on the gains, you can't claim the losses either. So, don't go hog wild in this investment.

2. You can take the money out one year, but you can't put it back in the same year. You can put it back in the following year or years.

3. You don't have to choose between a TFSA or RRSP. You can contribute to your RRSP, and the money you get back from the government you can then put into your TFSA.

In general, if you're saving your emergency fund outside of TFSA, you'll need to pay tax regularly as you buy and sell investments. You may avoid tax if your investments make money within the year you invested, but you'll need to keep outstanding records. Please consult your tax advisor or accountant on this matter.

CRA has strict rules. It's better to get the most up-to-date information and adhere to those rules.

- **Entertainment**

It's important to save for your vacation and any other entertainment fees. It will help you keep your money under control. I've already mentioned distinguishing between instant gratification and deferred gratification: Instant gratification means you'll be paying the bills after you get back from vacation; deferred gratification means you save for your holiday before you take it. One way adds stress, while the other brings peace of mind.

The other thing to keep in mind is gifting. Some families are very big gifters. That means, during birthdays and Christmas, people go into debt to buy expensive gifts. It might be best to spend quality time with family members and provide modest gifting ideas. Discuss this with your family members and make a rule for gifts at $10 or $20 per person. The whole idea regarding birthdays and holidays is to enjoy each other's company and not some pricy gifts.

• Education

Saving for your child's or grandchild's education is an excellent way to reduce their debt load. Typically, this money is in an RESP (Registered Education Savings Plan). You're using after-tax dollars to invest in the RESP. The great benefit here is that the government contributes a grant of up to $500 per year when you invest $2,500 (to a lifetime maximum of $7,200). There are no annual limits on your contributions, but there is a lifetime limit of $50,000 for each child. Also, when the child takes the money, they'll pay tax on the gains at a personal level, which will be much lower than your rate.

Note: It's important to realize that if the child doesn't want to go to post-secondary school, you'll have to return the government grant, and the growth in the investment will be taxed at your personal rate when you dissolve it. However, you have the option of using the money for another child, as long as they are under 21 and you opened a group RESP plan.

There's also the chance that the child will choose an education that costs a lot more than what you accumulated in the RESP. So, how can you provide for the possible shortfall?

- One way is to take out a universal life, whole life, or participating whole life policy on the child so that the money inside can grow tax-free.

- You could use OSAP (the child borrows money from the government).

- For an eligible child, there are also other grants available.

How to Use a Budget to Begin to Save

The rich always save first and spend the rest. The poor buy first and save the rest. Let's use the rich people's way. If you earn $3,000 per month, can you save $1, $2 or $3 per day? If you can save $1 a day, at the end of the month, you'll have approximately $30. In a year, you'll have $365. It doesn't sound like much, but in 10 years, you'll have $3,650 plus any investment gains. Proportionally for $2 a day, you'll have saved about $60 a month or $730 per year, and in 10 years, you'll have $7,200 plus investment gains. How about $3 a day? You'll save about $90 per month or $1,095 per year. In 10 years, you'll have accumulated $10,950 plus investment gains.

You can start small. Set up a budget for yourself, and don't deviate from it. Here's a sample of a simple budget.

Savings and Disposable Income

Income Saving	$4,000 $400 (10%)	$200 (5%)	$100 (2.5%)
Available to Spend	$3,600	$3,800	$3,900
Car Payment	$350	$350	$350
Rent	$1,700	$1,700	$1,700
Food	$700	$700	$700
Cell Phone	$75	$700	$700
Insurance	$350	$700	$700
Gas/ Bus Fare	$250	$700	$700
Clothing	$50	$700	$700
Miscellaneous	$125	$325	$425
What's Left	$0	$0	$0

Figure 7

The idea here is to limit your spending on unnecessary items. Paying loans, rent, and food are necessities, and you need to cover those first. When you get a raise or work on a part-time job, remember to adhere to this budget and save the extra cash.

CHAPTER 5

Investment Strategies (With and Without Life Insurance)

Where to Put the Money?

Once you have some money, you need to decide how to invest it. The decision as to where to put your money is equally important. Most people, including yours truly, try to invest for the greatest return. I didn't know about risk, but I certainly found out the hard way. Those big returns also come with significant risks. I didn't have the stomach for it and panicked. Well, you guessed it: I lost most of my money.

Instead of putting all of your money in one basket (i.e. real estate, stocks, or mortgages), why not diversify? Put a percentage of your money in real estate, stocks/bonds/mutual funds, private lending, business ventures, life insurance, seg funds, etcetera. Your choices should depend on your age and what you intend to do with your estate when you retire and when you die; the investment should be in line with your plans.

Chinese people love to buy real estate. There's nothing wrong with that. I'm Chinese, and I love real estate. If I had my way, I would probably own ten houses by now. However, I concluded that real estate has a fundamental problem: it isn't very liquid. That means I can't decide to sell it today and get my money tomorrow. There's a waiting period to get your funds out of real estate. Also, outside of my primary home, there's a 50% capital gains tax in Canada. So, if I have ten houses, one of which is my primary home that isn't taxed, the other nine buildings are taxable. When I die, my beneficiaries will need to come up with steep taxes for nine houses before the government releases those properties for sale. That imposes a huge burden on my beneficiaries. Also, until they're sold, my heirs will have to continue to look after my nine properties—with maintenance, property tax, utilities, and tenants. It's not a fun job. Do your children want this kind of hassle before they get their inheritance?

What about stocks, bonds, and mutual funds? They're more liquid. However, the day I pass away, the government deems them disposed of. That means they're sold regardless of market conditions. In April this year, during COVID-19, a good friend of mine died suddenly. He had much of his investments in stocks, bonds, and mutual funds, and the market had dropped 30-40%. Luckily, his wife inherited all. I hate to think what his heirs would finally have received if the investments had passed into their hands.

I've invested in syndicated mortgages as well as private lending—neither turned out as expected. The interest returns were good at 8% and 12%, but a borrower decided that he couldn't afford to pay, so he didn't. I lost quite a bit of money.

When I was laid off, many new grads approached me, and they asked me to help them with getting their first job. I decided to create a company to develop software to bring people nearby into restaurants and stores. I had never been an entrepreneur before, but it sounded really appealing. The project went well, but we failed in our marketing efforts. For development, I put in approximately $25K. It was a great lesson: I built it, and they didn't come (although I think it may still be a viable project for after COVID-19 when restaurants and stores need to re-introduce themselves to the public). As part of the project, I helped 20 students get their first job. It was worth it to see their happy faces as they moved on with their lives. I'm grateful to Ryerson University for providing the much needed office space and guidance.

* * *

Most people tell you all about things that went well and all the money they made during their lifetime, and, of course, I did have some money-making ventures. My husband and I made some money in real estate when we sold our house of 15 years in 2019. We also made some money in the stock market and private lending. I should note that my husband worked in the mutual fund industry, but he bought mostly bonds and GICs for his RRSP portfolio. According to him, mutual funds didn't make money. So he decided to become a GIC refugee.

In 1995, a London Life salesman approached me. He was polite, and he showed me how I could use whole life insurance as an investment tool. The illustration indicated they had 15% year-over-year returns. To me, that was good. I put in approximately $1,000 per month at the time for 20 years of participating life. I didn't know what I had bought with absolute certainty, and every time I paid the premium, my husband would complain. I finally couldn't stand it anymore, and—after 15 years of paying premiums—I stopped contributing. Today, that policy has more than doubled in size, and there has been no tax. Although the life insurance never gave me the 15% return depicted in the illustration, it forced me to save. Over the years, I've bought more life insurance, and each policy has helped me save more money.

I've since cashed in all but the first of those policies. And I also bought a different kind of life insurance so that I could control the investment. The reason for this is that you have no control over whole life insurance policy investments, which turned out to be problematic as my original purchase gave me less than a two percent return. That's a bit too low for me.

And I've pretty much resorted to using segregated funds for my RRSP, Non-Registered, and TFSA accounts. These are market-based investments (offered by a life insurance company) structured as a deferred variable annuity offering capital appreciation and death benefits to policyholders. The reasoning is that:

1. My beneficiaries will get my money within 5-10 business days of my death, AND it doesn't have to go through probate (a process where the courts validate the will at the cost of 0.5% to 1.5% of the estate's value).

2. Another great benefit is that the money is protected against any claims and lawsuits. If I ever get sued, the segregated funds I set up years ago won't be affected. Don't try to do this just before your court case because they will catch on and force you to give it up. The same goes for bankruptcy; you can't salt away money or get rid of substantial assets like real estate immediately before declaring bankruptcy (within two years before the event). You'll end up having to pay the current market value of the dissolved asset to your trustee.

3. My beneficiaries won't be the ones paying the capital gains tax, which can be substantial.

4. Depending on which segregated fund company I invested with, I can lock in the highest value of my investments each year. Then, if the market drops below that dollar amount and I die, my beneficiaries will get the greater of what I originally put into the vehicle or the last locked-in investment value. Another friend who died in 2020 left his children the market value of his stock, bonds, and mutual funds, which was 30-40% lower than what they would have gotten if he'd bought segregated funds. He also

left his wife with some real worries about where the market was when he passed away.

5. I also believe segregated funds are a safe way to invest in a trust for minor, mentally challenged and infirm relatives.

Some things to consider when you invest are:

1. How much time will it take to liquidate?

2. Who'll pay the tax when you die?

3. How much tax will the government take?

4. Do you want it to go through probate?

5. Will the beneficiaries be capable of managing the asset?

Wealth Protection

Formally, wealth protection is about planning for tomorrow so you can retain more of your assets, protect your estate, and leave a lasting legacy for your family. When looking at wealth protection, the key is to make sure the money grows safely. If you just park it in a bank or some low-interest vehicle, inflation and fees can eat away at your principal.

Some people invest in the stock market, while others buy real estate. Both have their up side and down side. And buying GICs at 3/4% just doesn't make sense. So, let's take baby steps and see where you can put your money so that you're naturally and safely saving a minimum of $1-$5 per day, $7-$35 per week, or $30-$140 per month.

When I was growing up, I had most of my money in the bank. Even after I learned about RRSPs and funnelled cash to that vehicle, I had some money left over in the bank account.

Of course, you can spend extra money on something like bitcoin. There are many investment vehicles with the potential to make more money for you, but that may not be the right way to build your estate.

I used to put my money in the stock market, hoping to cash in a big payoff. It never happened. I may have made a few hundred dollars here and there but never did hundreds of thousands of dollars fly my way. Why is that? It was because I don't know how the market works, and I wasn't patient enough to leave the money in there and let it grow.

So, maybe you're smarter. Perhaps you're a scholar of investment and more patient than me. All I can do is give you my opinion: I believe investing in the stock market isn't the way for a novice or someone with a weak stomach to grow their savings.

If you want to invest, I suggest that you start with the safest way recommended, focusing on protection first, carrying on with your fixed expenses and then supporting your lifestyle within your designated risk factor. That way, you're always going to have some money to fall back on.

For further information regarding your risk factor and investing in general contact me at **AMoneyMasterMillionaire.com**

What's the Secret to Growing Money?

The secret to growing your money is to be a savvy saver and investor, which is more easily said than done. I tried to follow some smart investors, but the market had moved by the time their newsletter came out. For example, when professionals bought a stock at $9 per share, I bought at $9.50 or $10.00. That's part of the profits I'll never realize. I've also taken many classes to become a better stock market investor, but I failed miserably. What I found is that I'm an average stock investor. My knowledge and resources are too limited. I can't compete with the professional investors who have armies of people doing research and can act quickly on buy and sell transactions. Therefore, I believe investing at regular intervals (i.e. on Mondays, weekly) will help even out the market's ups and downs. This method for buying a little bit at fixed intervals is called **Dollar Cost Averaging (DCA)**. Here's an example:

DCA is an <u>investment strategy</u> that aims to reduce the impact of <u>volatility</u> on large purchases of financial assets such as equities. By dividing the total sum to be invested in the market (e.g., $100,000) into equal amounts that are put into the market at regular intervals (e.g., $1,000 per week over 100 weeks), dollar cost averaging seeks to reduce the risk of incurring a substantial loss resulting from investing the entire lump sum just before a fall in the market.

Note: DCA is not always the most profitable way to invest a large sum, but it's used to try and minimize <u>downside risk</u>. The technique is said to work in markets undergoing temporary declines because it exposes only part of the total sum to the decline. The technique is so-called because of its potential for reducing the average cost of shares bought. As the number of shares that can be bought for a fixed amount of money varies inversely with their price, DCA effectively leads to more shares being purchased when their price is low, and fewer when they are expensive. As a result, the technique has the potential to lower the total average *cost per share* of the investment, giving the investor a lower overall cost for the shares purchased over time. DCA works best during a volatile market. The theory behind DCA is that while the market never goes straight up, it does trend upward over time.

However, there is also evidence against DCA. It doesn't work when the market goes up day after day, month after month, and year after year. Finance journalist Dan Kadlec of *Time* summarized the relevant research in 2012, writing: "The superior long-term returns of lump sum investing [over dollar cost averaging] have been acknowledged for more than 30 years." Similarly, decades of empirical research on DCA have found that it generally doesn't function as promoted and is usually a sub-optimal investment strategy.

Some investment advisors who acknowledge the sub-optimality of DCA nevertheless advocate it as a behavioural tool that makes it easier for some investors to start investing a lump sum. They contrast the relative benefits of DCA versus never investing the lump sum.

In summary, we all like to buy low and sell high. But greed and fear take over us, and we end up buying high and selling low. As you can see, with volatile markets, the dollar cost of averaging is probably the best defensive investing method. The only thing is if the market goes straight up, the average dollar cost of shares will result in a lower return. But since we can't predict future markets, I resort to DCA even though I won't earn as much in a booming market. I think it's better than losing my principal.

The Grass is Always Greener on the Other Side

Once I win in a few investments, I feel more confident in the market. Of course, I put more and more into each trade. Inevitably, I discover a better performing stock and want to shift my money to that. Why not? It will get me a better return. So, I sell my current position and buy the more attractive stock. The minute I purchase it, the stock starts to drop and drop and drop. This happens to me because I chase after profit; I forget about my investment plan.

There was a time when my investment plan told me to sell if I lost 50%. But I decided to stay in because I felt the stock would come back. Well, it didn't. It went to zero. What did I do? I swept the whole experience under the carpet and never talked about it. I just concentrated on those stocks that were making money. I even sold one stock so that I could tell people I'm a good investor who made 25% on one stock. Little did they know I lost $10,000 on my other investments.

Are you like that? Be honest. And remember I know how you feel. I've been there, and there's no shame in it. Just don't continue to maintain that investment pattern, or you'll lose all your investment dollars. Stop! Stop! Stop! Try the DCA method in segregated funds. You can sleep better, and, over time, your investments will grow.

Just remember, people never tell you how much they've lost. I never hear anyone say that they've lost their shirt, and now they have to sell their house. What I do see is people who'll start living at their friends' house or sleeping on the couch or in their car.

Investing in Real Estate

Everyone needs a place to live, and it's ideal to own a place to live, which I refer to as the primary home or residence. The Canadian government provides incentives to own your primary home by allowing you to borrow from your RRSP as a first-time homebuyer. Also, when you sell your primary residence, there's no tax.

The most challenging aspect of buying your first home is to come up with a down payment. In Toronto, the average one-bedroom condo is approximately $450K, a three-bedroom townhouse is over $900K, and a three-bedroom single house is in the neighbourhood of $1.35M. Coming up with a $100-$300K down payment isn't easy. And once you buy the home, it becomes stressful for you to continuously make the monthly mortgage, maintenance, utility, and tax payment, especially when the job market isn't stable.

So, how can you get started? Buying something affordable would be ideal. Plan it out carefully. Make sure you have some emergency funds ready and available.

If you're looking outside of Ontario and British Columbia, the housing price is more reasonable. However, it becomes more difficult to find a job, and the marketplace may not support a quick sale. My brother bought his home in Alberta in early 2000, when he moved there. The house hasn't gained much investment value. In fact, the price dropped due to the falling of natural resources. I wouldn't take housing price increases for granted even if you're living in Ontario and British Columbia, where housing is hot; some markets are going up very slowly or haven't moved at all.

With COVID-19, the government will be looking for places where they can get extra tax dollars. A capital gains tax increase from 50% to 75% is a possibility. Government can also increase property tax. An increase in HST from 13% is another possibility. Also, we're currently enjoying primary homes not being taxed at all. In the future, they may very well be subject to tax. Lastly, the interest rate is at a record low. If the interest rate goes up, the housing prices might fall as people won't be able to afford to carry their properties.

Already, downtown condos are sitting empty as students and office workers are studying and working from home. How will this impact the resale value of these properties? It's important to consider this, as well as travel restrictions on any Airbnb rental properties. Once the government subsidy ends, those without positive cash flow will be in distress, so the prices will fall. How far? No one knows for sure. My guess is it will be substantial. If the interest rate rises by even 1% during this situation, many will go bankrupt and need refinancing.

Commercial real estate is usually a good investment option. However, with COVID-19, commercial properties are losing a bit of value as people aren't going to work, and many businesses have decided to continue to work from home. Office spaces in downtown Toronto are empty. When government rental subsidies end, we'll find out what commercial properties are actually worth.

Investing in Stocks

When people have some money, the first thing they often do is do some stock speculation. With that, they have more of a risk of losing their savings than gaining. The following chart indicates what place speculation has in the larger scheme of things.

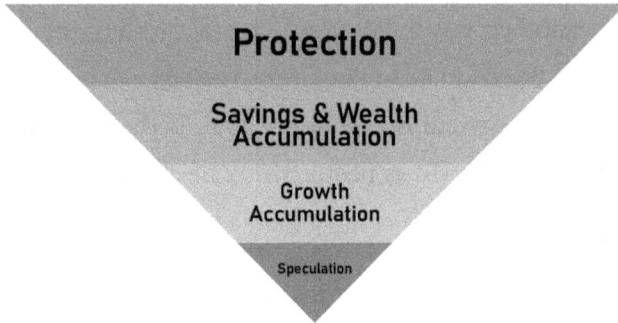

Figure 8

Many people have made huge amounts of money in the stock market. Sir John Templeton was a legendary investor and mutual fund manager who founded the Templeton Growth Fund. He was an early innovator in global value investing, and his family of funds held more than **$13 billion** in assets when he sold the firm in 1992. Warren Buffett is an American investor, business tycoon, philanthropist and Chairman and CEO of Berkshire Hathaway. He's also one of the richest men in the world. And billionaires George Soros, Paul Tudor Jones II, John Paulson, Andreas Halvorsen and Bill Ackerman are all stock traders.

However, the majority of people lose in the stock market—including yours truly. Don't get me wrong; I made quite a bit of money in Microsoft, Dell, Cisco, and Apple early on, but outside of these market darlings I had many losers as well.

It's getting harder and harder to make money in the stock market because of auto-trader software. If you aren't using this kind of software, it may be something you want to consider. Personally, I wouldn't want to trust a computer program with my hard-earned dollars, but if you're trading, finding a reputable company and sticking to it may be the route for you.

When you start to save and have a few dollars in your savings account, it's very tempting to use that money to invest. I don't blame you because that's how I got started. I heard about all kinds of people making huge returns, so I ventured that way when I was in my 20s and 30s (the 1980s and 1990s). The market didn't treat me as nice as my friends. Or so I thought. They seemed to be making money but, somehow, I kept losing money. I took course after course, finally started to make money, then something happened to the economy. I lost all the money I'd gained and then some. It was very difficult for me to determine when to stay in for the long term.

Many people stayed put when Nortel fell from its grace; lots of money lost there. My father-in-law also got sucked in by Bre-X. So, how can you and I know when to sell and when to buy? Well, we don't. We're mainly a bunch of sheep following the crowd. I seem to get wind of stocks just before their tipping point, and then I end up losing my investments. So, if you're like me and don't want to invest in the stock market today, I understand. What, then, are the alternatives?

I'll always remember my trading class teacher saying, "The trend is your friend until the end." He meant if you're trading because the market is either trending up or down, you'll do well except when it turns the other way. The point is that you can count on one thing: The market will change direction, and, at that point, the trend becomes your enemy. Be careful!

Investing in Foreign Exchange (FOREX)

In the 2000s, I ventured into Foreign Exchange trading, which is an unregulated market.

I'm so sorry that I got a good friend of mine into this field. She was very smart, and with her little bit of investment, she said she almost made $1 million. One night when she was trading a very large sum, her application froze, and she couldn't come out of her trade. She lost everything. She complained, but nothing ever happened.

Then there was the time when I put in a trade with a very low stop. The Canadian dollar dipped to just that point and bounced back. I lost all my money. What are the chances that the USD/EUR pair would drop to 300 pips? The company that ran the foreign exchange denies any wrongdoing. However, it seems the company had an inside track on who put in low stops, and so the market would drop to that point just to pick up your low stops. It's called fishing and trolling, which is illegal, but foreign exchange companies weren't in a regulated market at the time, and so anything went. Watch out for these tricks.

Many people only trade a few pips at a time, so they get in and—once they've reached their trading plan—get out. It's not a bad way to go. I did this for three months and consistently made money at it. **Note:** A pip, which is short for "percentage in point" or "price interest point," represents a small, standardized measure of the change in a pair of currencies in the foreign exchange market. It's usually $0.0001 (1/100th of 1% or one basis point) for USD related currency pairs. The extremely small pip helps to protect investors from huge losses by reducing the volatility in currency prices.

Before you start trading FOREX, I'd suggest that you take a course from a reputable company and learn from the professionals. It will be worth your while to learn how to read historical charts and know when the news will be coming out. Stay away from trading when there are significant economic announcements. Even most experienced traders will tell you to stay away because a split second's volatility can wipe you out. Go with diligent caution and care.

*   *   *

There are a ton of books about investing. Which strategy would you believe and adopt? It's a million-dollar question. They all work to some extent—until they don't work any longer. So, you find another strategy, and then another strategy. Eventually, you're so confused (like I was) you resort to GICs. Remember the example of my husband who worked for a mutual fund company, yet most of his investments are in GICs and bonds? He's an example of a Fixed Income Refugee.

Investing in Mortgages / Syndicated Mortgages

To invest in mortgages as the lender, you go through a broker to get a borrower. You can be the first, second, or third mortgager for the money you lend, although the bank is most likely to be the primary mortgage holder. The risk here is that if the housing price drops and the house's selling price is just enough to pay for the loan from the first mortgager (the bank), then you would lose your money. However, if the borrower does repay you, the interest is typically more than what you would get from putting your money in the bank. So, as long as the housing price keeps going up, the risk of holding a second or third mortgage is minimal. By selling the property, you can always get your money back.

* * *

A few years back, I met up with a business associate of mine. He was very smart in investing and introduced me to syndicated mortgages. A syndicated mortgage is one where many investors lend a small amount of money to a company for a project. That could be building houses, constructing a commercial building, or finishing a project. The intent here is that each would receive a healthy return on investment. The syndicated mortgage I participated in was supposed to give me an 8% return. It didn't. I lost money.

You see, I didn't know that this type of mortgage investment can be extremely risky. I was told they're security instruments governed by the Financial Services Commission of Ontario (FSCO). However, syndicated mortgages are currently sold by licensed mortgage brokers and have historically been exempted from the standard registration and filing provisions related to the sale and distribution of a security.

I was blinded by loyalty to my friend, and I didn't do enough investigation. Syndicated Mortgage Investments (SMIs) were sold to me as "low risk, high reward," which belies the actual and often not appreciated dangers of relying on loans offered by issuers with repayment dependent on future financing and development.

FSCO has seen an increase in complaints about syndicated mortgages over the last five years. Some of these complaints have received media attention. In particular, Fortress Real Developments Inc. (one of the largest companies in the syndicated mortgage industry) was named in four proposed class-action lawsuits in 2016 along with FSCO. The suits claimed $27.5 million in damages and a return of any profits for a condominium development project in Barrie, Ontario. The lawsuits alleged that Fortress, its principals, and its related entities misled investors by representing that the development project was "safe and secure." In particular, the investors claimed they were kept in the dark regarding how their money was spent and the land's real value.

Yours truly was introduced to Fortress, and that's where I parked a good chunk of my RRSP. I lost on two different projects. I recovered one of the investments, but the other is still in court.

Cash, Mutual Funds, and Segregated Funds

I invested in mutual funds for many years because my advisor insisted that it would increase my wealth. Of course, I was informed I had to keep it there forever and never touch it. The investments went up and then came down and repeated that cycle over and over again. I didn't make much money. After 20+ years, I was tired of it, so I cashed out and bought a bigger primary home. That was a great deal because 15 years later, we sold our home and made 300+ percent tax-free.

After we moved to a condo near my mother-in-law to take better care of her, there was a good chunk of money left over from the sale of our home, and that left us wondering where to invest next. Luckily, we were introduced to segregated funds, which have been around for decades. The reason they weren't popular in the past is that the interest rate was high. Why invest in a segregated fund when you can put your money in the bank at 24%—as was the case in the 80s? I remember paying $1,500 per month on my mortgage, and at the end of the year, I had only paid $100 in principal. Ouch.

What are segregated funds? They're like mutual funds, but with two major guarantees:

1. Maturity guarantees

    a) Segregated funds typically mature in 10-15 years. Some are contract-based (from the date the contract is opened). Some are deposit-based (after each deposit, the contract is extended 10-15 years).

    b) If a segregated fund value drops in the year of maturity, you can still get the last locked-in price.

2. Death guarantees

    a) You can reset the guaranteed value of your contract when the market value exceeds the original value of your investment, allowing you to lock in market growth. So, if the market tanks on the day you pass away, your beneficiaries will receive the last locked-in value tax-free.

Life Insurance, Critical Illness and Long-Term Care

Before you take your hard-earned dollar into the stock market, consider protecting your earning potential. The most important thing in the house is not the house itself but rather the people who live in it. You insure just about everything (car, home, travel, pet), but most people never think about insuring themselves. When you have an accident or the primary income earner or spouse dies or gets sick, the whole family's financial situation becomes extremely stressful. So, I suggest you build your financial house right, with protection being the main foundation.

If you work for a company as an employee, you may have life insurance worth one or two times your salary. At best, that would cover expenses for one or two years. What happens after that time? Where is your family going to get financial support?

You may also have disability insurance (which provides partial wage replacement when you experience an injury or illness) and critical insurance (which pays a specified amount when you experience certain illnesses like cancer) through work. But these vehicles will only replace part of your earning potential. It would be best to explore ways of creating a fund you or your family can access when the need arises.

Speculation

Growth
Accumulation

Savings & Wealth
Accumulation

Protection

Figure 9

Note: You don't purchase life insurance, disability insurance, and critical illness insurance to make someone rich. You buy it to cover expenses so that your family can survive financially after disaster strikes. It should replace the earnings they expected you to provide had you lived.

*   *   *

Part of a solid protection plan is ensuring your family doesn't lose the home because you die or are unable to work. There are three types of insurance that can protect you in these situations:

1. **Mortgage loan insurance (post-claim underwriting)**

   This is a policy that actually protects the bank in case of loan default, which means the insurance claim amount must be used to pay off your loan to the bank. It's important to understand that with this type of insurance underwriting happens when the claim is made, and you may not qualify. Should that happen, you're still responsible for the mortgage loan and could lose the house.

2. **Mortgage life insurance (post-claim underwriting)**

   This is life insurance that pays off the mortgage in the event of your death. The amount of coverage may or may not decrease as what you owe decreases, depending on the type of policy. As in the previous example, the underwriting happens when the claim is made, so you may not qualify. If that happens, your spouse or estate will have to assume the mortgage.

3. **Personal life insurance (pre-claim underwriting)**

   This is life insurance that exists independent of your mortgage. It can cover the amount of your mortgage and some additional money for your loved ones. Since this type of insurance is underwritten when you apply for the policy, your spouse or estate will get the claimed amount should you die.

It's crucial you understand that even though you fill out an insurance application form, you and your family may not be protected, especially if the insurance is subject to "post-claim underwriting." Always read through your policies and ask questions so that you're clear about what you're paying for. My suggestion is that if you can get pre-claim underwriting, do so.

> Check out this CBC Youtube video
> **https://www.youtube.com/watch?v=rmzWz_t0IpU.**

Pandemic Impact

In 2020, the unprecedented COVID-19 pandemic hit many families hard. I'm very sorry to see them suffering through this disaster, but the time to prepare is before such things happen. And this won't be the last disaster to come our way. Do something now to protect your family from financial woe so that your future self will thank you for it.

Top Life Insurance Myths Revealed

I don't need coverage because I'm single and don't have dependents. Even single people need at least enough life insurance to cover the costs of personal debts, medical bills, and funeral expenses, so their family doesn't have to pick up the tab. Some people also use life insurance as a low-cost way to leave something to a favourite charity or other cause.

My life insurance coverage only needs to be twice my annual salary. If you have dependents, life insurance should cover your annual salary for as many years as you expect them to need your earnings. A cash flow or needs analysis is usually necessary to determine the amount of life insurance you need to purchase.

My term life insurance coverage at work is sufficient. This is typically one or two times your annual salary. That may be enough if you're single and have minimal debt. But what happens to a family with complex needs extending over a long period?

The cost of my premiums will be deductible. Because life insurance benefits are tax-free, you must usually pay the premiums with after-tax dollars. One exception is that the cost of personal life insurance is deductible when the policyholder is self-employed, and the benefit is to be used as asset protection for the business owner.

I must have life insurance at any cost. You should only buy life insurance if the decision makes financial sense. For example, people with substantial assets and no debt or dependents may be better off self-insuring. Also, if you have medical and funeral costs covered, life insurance coverage may be optional. When in doubt, talk to your accountant.

I should always buy term and invest the difference. You should invest in what makes sense for your financial risk profile. A good accountant or financial representative can help you determine such a profile. Also, there are distinct differences between term life and permanent life insurance. For example, while the cost of term life coverage may seem attractive, the premiums can become prohibitively high later. Therefore, if you know with certainty that you must be covered at death, permanent coverage is probably the most cost-efficient choice. There's also the risk of non-insurability to consider, which could be disastrous if you have estate tax issues and will need life insurance to pay them. The choice here would be permanent coverage, which becomes paid up after a certain amount of premium has been paid and remains in force until death.

I'm better off investing my money than buying life insurance of any kind. Hogwash! Until you reach the break-even point of asset accumulation, you need life insurance coverage of some sort. For example, once you amass $1,000,000 of liquid assets, you can consider whether to discontinue or reduce your million-dollar policy. Letting the policy go before this puts your family at risk.

A word about the difference between variable universal life policies and straight universal life policies: Many universal policies pay competitive interest rates, but variable universal life (VUL) policies contain several layers of fees relating to both the insurance and securities elements present in the policy. If the policy's variable aspects don't perform well, the policyholder may see a lower cash value than someone with a straight universal life policy (UL).

Poor market performance can even require additional premiums to be paid to keep the variable policy in force. Ouch again!

In Conclusion

The key is to build the cost of life insurance into your budget until you have enough assets to cover your expenses after you're gone. Speak to your trusted financial planner to determine the amount of insurance that's right for you or contact me at **AMoneyMasterMillionaire.com**

CHAPTER 6

Tax Implications

To become a great money master millionaire, you need to pay particular attention to the amount of tax you pay each year and prepare for when you pass away. That's when your portfolio structure for minimum taxation of your estate can make a huge difference. You may say you don't care how much money the government takes when you pass away, but after spending your lifetime accumulating hard-earned dollars, why not do some good with the money? I suggest planning so that your estate doesn't lose over half of its value to taxes. You can give the money to a charity, your beneficiaries, or organizations that will do good.

I suggest that since taxation impacts most products offered by financial institutions, you should consider it an integral part of an investment and hence your financial decision-making.

I believe there can be four investment piles:

1. **Taxable:** You create this type of investment pile with after-tax dollars. The government will take a portion of the gain each time you sell any investment not given special consideration by the government.

2. **Tax-Deferred (Type 1):** This type of pile is funded with before-tax dollars and grows tax-free. The government will tax the money as it's used, presumably at a lower income tax rate than when you put it in. The investment vehicle is called a Registered Retirement Savings Plan (RRSP).

3. **Tax-Deferred (Type 2):** You seed this type of investment pile with after-tax money, but the growth is taxed at the user's (your children's) lower income level. This investment vehicle is called a Registered Education Savings Plan (RESP).

4. **Tax-Advantaged:** This last money pile also accumulates after-tax money, but when you use it, the growth won't be taxed (also known as non-taxable).

As a money master millionaire, you want to slowly move your money from taxable to tax-deferred to tax-advantaged vehicles. The example provided in Chapter Four illustrates the types of investments that are taxable, tax-deferred and tax-advantaged (non-taxable).

To illustrate with a specific example, let's assume you have $50,000 before-tax dollars to invest:

For pile 1 (Taxable), you'll only have $40,000 to invest because $10,000 is lost to taxes. Also, in most cases, you'll pay tax yearly as your investment increases in value or when you sell your investment.

For pile 2 (Tax-deferred Type 1), you'll have $50,000 to invest (assuming you have room left in your RRSP to put the $50,000). You won't have to pay tax on the gains, but you'll have to pay tax when you use the money at your personal income tax rate. The more you withdraw, the more tax you'll have to pay.

For pile 3 (Tax-deferred Type 2), you'll have $40,000 to invest. You won't have to pay tax on the gains, but your children will pay tax when they use the money at their income tax rate for education. If your child doesn't go to school, the growth will be 100% taxable at your income tax rate.

For pile 4 (Tax-advantaged), you'll have $40,000 invest, but you don't have to pay tax on the gains. In this pile, you can use a TFSA, universal life, or whole life insurance policies.

Now, assuming you can get a 5% return on the investments just mentioned: for 20 and 40 years, the table below shows the money that's available for you to use…

Category	1 (Non-Registered)	2 (RRSP)	3 (RESP)	4 (TFSA * / Universal Life **/Whole Life **)
	Taxable	Tax-Deferred (1)	Tax-Deferred (2)	Tax-Advantaged
Income	$300,000			
Invest	$40,000 After Tax	$50,000 Before Tax	$40,000 After Tax	$40,000 After Tax
Insurance face value				$500,000 Your child age 1: Male
After 20 years	$91,010/25	$132,665	$106,132	$86,691
After 40 years	$205,684	$319,274	268,190	$220,916 with insurance face value of $767,846 ***
Taxation	No	Yes	Yes—at your child's income rate	No, if withdrawing less than 90% No, if you are borrowing against it
Policy Rules	* No withdrawal restrictions but cannot put it back in the same year ** Subjected to your life insurance policy withdrawal and borrow limit. Will be subjected to income tax if withdrawing more than 90% *** Insurance face value is what the beneficiaries will get if something happens to the insured.			

Figure 10

Just remember that tax planning isn't a separate function from which you can exclude yourself. As a money master millionaire, your investment and financial decisions aren't made for tax reasons only, but ignoring them can lead to poor choices that fail to maximize after-tax wealth.

I'll go a step further and say that tax constitutes a predominant factor in the accumulation and preservation of wealth. It's critical to sound personal financial planning because budgeting, protection, investments, retirement, estate planning, and emergency fund generation involve after-tax cash flows. You're taxed when you earn money; you're taxed when you spend money; and most of all, you're taxed when you pass away. Tax is cancer to wealth building.

> **In Canada, there are two levels of taxes:**
> **Federal Tax and Provincial Tax.**
> **Visit https://www.Canada.ca**

It's worth your while to know something about taxation. You can take an introductory taxation course, or you can pick up a good taxation book. This way, you're aware of what's important. However, to be good at it and keep up to date will take some effort. There are 1,500 pages of taxation rules to keep track of, and that's a full-time job.

A friend of mine insisted on doing his taxes. He spent three to four months every year on the practice. Then, he never bothered to file his tax over the last few years, and he paid many penalties. How unnecessary. You can leverage a good tax accountant to help you plan your tax strategies; it can help you save time and money, and that's worth the cost. Also, review your plan periodically or whenever you have a dramatic change in your life, such as getting married or divorced, having kids or grandkids, moving to a new place, etc.

My second husband never had any tax education, but he wanted to do our taxes. I was young and naïve back then, and I let him do so. I had just started my own consulting business at the time, and he filed our income tax without doing income distribution. After the divorce, I took our income tax to an accountant. He was able to claim back a lot of money just by doing back taxes on income distribution. You can know one rule, but what about a thousand other laws? Hire a good tax accountant to file your tax. Delegate this task to the professionals.

Tax Implications for Businesses

When you own a business, the government provides you with tax credits and incentives to help lower costs, hire/train workers, compete in the marketplace, and support various sectors.

For example: Refundable tax credits are available to employers who hire and train apprentices in certain skilled trades and eligible university or college students enrolled in a recognized post-secondary co-operative education program. A new refundable corporate income tax credit is available in Ontario to support businesses that construct, renovate, or acquire eligible commercial and industrial buildings in designated regions across the province. And Ontario parallels the federal government in allowing businesses to accelerate write-offs of capital investments. Also, if you're a home-based business, you can deduct a portion of your house expenses from your business income.

I'll again stress the importance of securing a good accountant to help you navigate the tax waters. I had an online business. My husband was my bookkeeper, and he helped with GST and HST. To do the job quickly, he tallied up all my expenses and then did a one-time entry. That caused a bit of a problem because he didn't know I had personal items embedded in the receipts. I was audited by the CRA and had to repay a couple of thousands of dollars of miscategorized GST. It was my fault for not keeping my business purchases separate from personal expenses. In the end, it also caused me an additional 25% to pay for an accountant who helped me with my audit.

The tax lessons I learned are to keep personal purchases separate from your business, maintain good records, and hire a professional accountant <u>before</u> you get into trouble.

Tax Implications for Family Trusts

In Canada, you can save on taxes by starting a family trust.

A family trust is an excellent way to split income with family members who are the trust beneficiaries. Income splitting involves transferring income from a high-income earner to a low-income earner. It's an effective way to reduce family taxes because low-income earners pay less tax.

Examples of income splitting through a trust include:

- Profits from real estate investments

- Profits from a business

- Profits from stocks and bonds

You can also multiply the capital gains exemption on the sale of private company shares using a family trust. In Canada, the first $800,000 of profit on the sale of private company shares can be protected from taxation by using the capital gains exemption. This exemption is available to each beneficiary of a properly structured family trust. See the diagram on the next page...

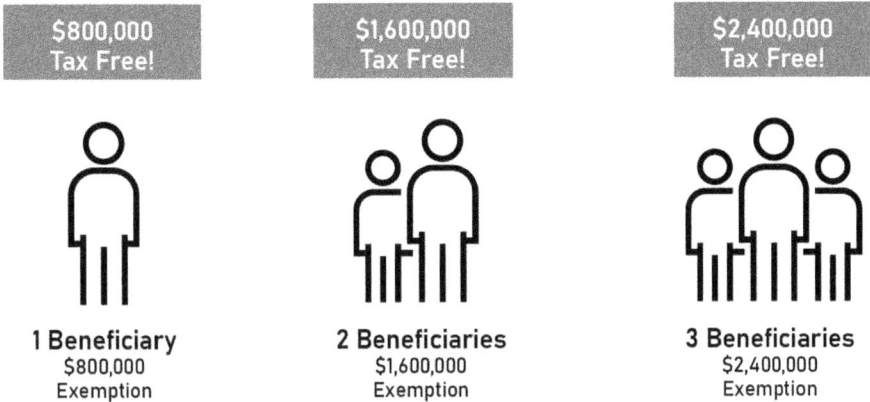

$800,000 Tax Free!	$1,600,000 Tax Free!	$2,400,000 Tax Free!
1 Beneficiary $800,000 Exemption	**2 Beneficiaries** $1,600,000 Exemption	**3 Beneficiaries** $2,400,000 Exemption

Figure 11

As you can see, the setup of a family trust in Canada isn't complicated but still requires a professional tax accountant to ensure you create it in compliance with applicable trust laws.

Tax Implications for RRSPs and TFSAs

Let's face it; there are very few programs that provide you with tax-free incentives. RRSPs (Registered Retirement Savings Plans) and TFSAs (Tax-Free Savings Accounts) are the two government incentive programs that can give you some tax relief. Use them to the max.

For TFSAs, there's a yearly limited contribution amount. However, you can use any of the contribution room from prior years. Most people put their money in the bank and don't even bother to create a TFSA because either the yearly contribution amount ceiling is too low, or they haven't got around to it. It's a shame because you are losing out on keeping the gains to yourself.

Money gained outside of this account is taxable. Albeit it's a small amount, but it does accumulate over the years. So start now, open a TFSA and put your extra money in this account. A lot of people use this account as an emergency fund. It's great because you can take money out when you need it, and you can replace it in the following year.

What about RRSPs? If you're earning more than the minimum $45K per year, I'd say you should put some money away for your retirement in a RRSP. The tax saving during the contribution year and the tax-free gain in subsequent years are benefits that can help you with a better retirement. However, using your RRSP as part of a risky investment fund can backfire: Just as you don't need to report gains in your RRSP, you can't report losses. So if you put your RRSP in high-risk investments and lose it, you're out of luck. Also, you need to balance what goes into your RRSP, TFSA and non-registered accounts.

Note: If your employer matches what you contribute, then do participate. It's like giving yourself a raise. Then look at your RRSP threshold. If you can drop your income to the next lower level, you'll save tax on the amount of money put in and the amount of money you have to pay on the income. That's the best scenario.

For example, if you earn $50,000 per year and your employer matches your contribution up to 3%, you can save $1,500 per year while your employer will contribute $1,500. Now you'll have $3,000 in your RRSP account. But the government charges you 20% tax when you earn $45,000 or less and charges you 30% if you earn more than $45,000. So, what if you raised your contribution to $5,100 from earnings of $50,000? Now your income drops to $44,900, which means your income tax rate is only 20%. And you've managed to save $5,100 + $1,500 in your RRSP account.

If this confuses you, just talk to your trusted tax accountant. They can figure out what your optimum contribution threshold is.

Tax Implications for Real Estate

Owning property in Canada can be profitable if you understand where to buy properties, and the Canadian tax laws applicable to real estate investments.

Since there's no residency or citizenship requirement for buying and owning property in Canada, you can temporarily occupy a Canadian residence. You'll need to comply with immigration requirements if you wish to have an extended stay or become a permanent resident.

Non-residents can also own rental property in Canada, but you need to file annual tax returns with the Canada Revenue Agency (CRA). As a real estate investment, property taxes and interest expenses are tax-deductible. However, to invest profitably, you should be aware of the tax implications of every stage of the investment, from owning the property and inhabiting or renting it to eventually selling it.

There are other issues to consider:

With the increase of property transfer tax, the price of housing dropped slightly for a short period. The market has also been picking up speed because of low-interest rates. But things could easily change. For example, there's talk about how the Canadian government will need to raise taxes to pay for COVID-19 pandemic expenses. Increasing property tax or decreasing capital gains from 50% to 25% are possible ways the government could raise money.

There's still merit in buying a home, though. Renovating your primary residence is much easier (fewer city by-laws, for example) than working on commercial or rental properties. And the potential exists for more profit because you're adding equity to your net worth, and the gains on your property are tax-free. It's for this reason that I buy fixer-upper houses, live in them while I renovate, and then sell for tax-free profit.

Tax Implications for Life Insurance

"You have to make the shift from being a consumer in the economy to becoming an owner—and you do it by becoming an investor."
–Tony Robbins

The question when considering taxes is where to invest your money. Typically, a risk-averse person might put their money in GICs. But with low interest rates, such investment returns have been below the cost of living, resulting in lost buying power each year.

Recently, I was introduced to the segregated fund. It's a life insurance product where you're guaranteed your principal plus any locked-in gains. It has not one but two guarantees:

1. Maturity Guarantee: If I hold the money to maturity (10-15 years), I'm guaranteed my principal plus any gains I've locked in.

2. Death Benefit Guarantee: If the market tanks when I die, my beneficiaries will be guaranteed my principal plus any gains I've locked in.

This kind of investment is particularly suitable for RRSPs and TFSAs because you don't want to choose risky investments and not be able to claim a loss. And depending on which segregated fund you select, you can get pretty good returns. There are dogs out there, just like in mutual funds or real estate, so you have to be aware of the company and the type of funds you select.

The other major life insurance products available in Canada are Term, Term 100, Universal Life, Whole Life, and Participating Whole Life.

Category	Term	Term 100	Universal Life	Whole Life	Participating Whole Life
Expires	10-20-30 Years	To Age 100	To Age 100	To Age 100	To Age 100
Price	Seems Cheap	More Expensive than Term	The insurance portion is cheaper than Term	More expensive than Universal Life	More expensive than Whole Life
Investment			You and Your Adviser controlled	Company-controlled	Company-controlled
Payment	Fixed	Fixed	Variable	Fixed	
Payment Terms	Fixed	Fixed	Variable	Fixed	Fixed

Figure 12

I like universal life insurance. Term insurance has no investment component, and whole life doesn't seem to provide the same investment growth as does universal life. For example, I held participating whole life insurance for many years, and the insurance agent told me the product would give greater than an eight percent return. The first few years were just above seven percent. After that, it dropped to between three and four percent. Also, the guarantee that came with the policy was so low that it only covered 25% of what I put in. After 20+ years, even though the policy was paid up, I was in danger of losing money. I finally cashed it in and bought universal life insurance. My money began to grow again.

What I'm saying here is that as a money master millionaire, you'll need to select your investment vehicle carefully and adjust as you see fit. By continuing the way it was, the insurance policy I had would have eventually imploded. I would have needed to put more money in, or the policy would have expired—something that has happened to many people. Review your policy from time to time and compare it from year to year. You can also write to me at **AMoneyMasterMillionaire@gmail.com,** and I can help you review your policy.

A lot of people buy life insurance but don't fund it properly. What that means is that they only put in the minimum payment allowed. The problem with this is that most of that premium services the insurance rather than growing the investment. You see, whole life and universal life insurance products have two parts: 1) insurance and 2) investment. If you only put enough money in to cover the insurance portion, there's no investment in the insurance policy. So, when it comes to the end of your term, you have no cash value.

I recently made a comparison and found that the insurance inside a universal life policy is cheaper than term insurance by at least 20-25%. And, by over-funding the UL policy, you can get a solid cash value accumulating tax-free. Also, if you need money, you can borrow against the insurance policy, like using house equity. If you already own a primary home and want to invest in something safer, this is a vehicle you can consider. It's worth your time to investigate and understand.

CHAPTER 7

How Can You
Get Started

So, you now have some ideas regarding becoming a money master millionaire, but you probably don't know how to start the journey. Keep reading, and start work on each suggested activity. It may take a few hours, a day, a week, a month or more to do each task, depending on where you are on your journey. Everyone's different, so you need to set your own timeline. Log on at **AMoneyMasterMillionaire.com** to get started.

Building a Support Team

No one is good at everything all at once. But, you can start to take a preliminary assessment of what you know, what you want to know, and what you need to do. Let's say you want to create a trust and you're an accountant. It may not be worth your while to study to become a lawyer before you work on the trust, so you'll need to find one you can afford and have faith in. You get what I mean, right? You wouldn't buy a franchise restaurant just to feed yourself, so why would you think you can become a money master millionaire on your own?

And why do you need a preliminary assessment? Because what you think you need in the beginning may be different once you're in the middle or at the end of your financial strategic planning. For example, you'll probably need a different skillset five to ten years from now.

In general, if you aren't an accountant or lawyer, you might need such people to help you pull things together financially. If you're a savvy number person and know how to get around the legal system, you can save money by doing it yourself. But, if you're new at this, I'd suggest you hire someone in those areas, at least on an as-needed basis.

Here are the Steps to Follow to Be a Money Master Milliionaire

Step 1: Consolidate Your Assets and Tabulate Them in an Excel Spreadsheet or Write Them Down. Go to **AMoneyMasterMillionaire.com** to get your workbook. The assets can be business property or personal property. I suggest you keep two lists. Other things you can record here are your RRSP, TFSA and non-registered accounts. That includes your trading accounts, bank accounts, etc. You can also list your insurance policies. Note: If you have a term or term 100 policy, there will be no current market value (surrender value).

Step 2: Select a Financial Planner. Just like you need air, food, and water, you need to learn about finances. Society failed us by not teaching us how to manage money when we were young. I would suggest slowly learning how to plan yourself. However, when you first get started, you may need some help to ensure you've considered all aspects of your financial planning. That may mean you get involved with a financial institution or private financial planner (which may cost you). Once you engage them, they'll help you to decide on the type of investments you need. Note: If associated with a financial institution, they may only recommend their products. In that case, they're getting paid by you and the financial institution for which they work. For that reason, I prefer to use someone not associated with any particular investment company. Companies that don't have their own products are free to provide you with the most suitable products in the marketplace at the time. In the end, it's still your choice.

Using a financial planner will ensure six areas of your personal planning are discussed: budgeting, retirement, protection, emergency fund, education fund and estate planning.

Here are some key questions you may want to ask the financial planner you're considering:

Why are you doing this line of work?

1. Can you provide a disclosure document or tell me how you get paid?

   a) Salary + bonus

   b) Commission only

   c) A planning fee

2. Can you provide a list of testimonials?

3. How often should we meet after this initial planning phase?

4. Do you or can you recommend products I can purchase?

5. Do you provide personal financial strategy training sessions?

Step 3: Implement Your Plan. Actively implement your financial strategy after you've accounted for all your assets, liabilities, income, and expenses. Personal protection is a good foundation on which to build (see the chart below). Your future self and your family members will thank you should something happen to you along the way (knock on wood). The amount of protection you'll need typically ranges from two to ten times your income. The reason it should be higher when you're younger is because of the amount of debt you may be carrying, as well as the age of your spouse and your kids. The younger they are, the longer they'll need the income you provide and the more you'll need to have in terms of protection. That way, in your absence, they can continue to live the same lifestyle as if you were there. It will lessen the impact of your death.

Once you're protected, you can work on your savings and retirement (See diagram in Chapter Six). Just remember, it's not how much you make but rather how much you keep.

Step 4: Learn Personal Financial Strategy. It's fine to rely on someone else when you start your personal financial strategy phase. However, you need to pick up some knowledge on the way so you can consistently help yourself. And if you depend on your spouse, you might be left to do it on your own one day. So, start learning now. Financial planners can help.

I know many people can't be bothered with learning, or think they have enough knowledge. Since new products and services are being introduced all the time, it's essential as a money master millionaire that you stay on top of the learning curve and apply the ones that make sense to you and your family.

I didn't pick up on how to do my finances until later in life. As a result, I lost more than I gained. I suppose I didn't notice because I was earning a good income. Now, I'm very thankful to be plugged into a personal financial planning group. I've taken some essential personal finance classes and continuously get up-to-date information. I've also purchased online subscriptions from several institutions and private companies that tell me what to invest in. But I know now that personal financial planning is more than just investing your money in the stock market. It includes the six areas mentioned in Step 2. These are budgeting, retirement, protection, emergency fund, education fund, and estate planning. Can you do well with one or two of them missing? I suppose. But when the time comes for you to retire or when you reach the end of life, you'll noticeably miss having all the areas covered.

Over my lifetime, I've bought many assets and many insurance policies. I didn't have much of a clue regarding what I'd bought. Sure, I knew all the terms, but I didn't understand the implications. I read the information but didn't fully understand the various products or how to integrate one with another. Then a friend of mine introduced me to World Financial Group (WFG). I signed up to learn, and I got a lot of helpful information. I know there's Google, but can I always believe what I see online? Not likely. Some things have sounded convincing, so I tried them and lost money. Overall, I failed miserably.

WFG allows me to learn personal financial strategies and, in Canada, they provide me connections to 60+ providers and products that I can potentially review. I only buy once I understand what I'm buying and what's good for my family and me. I can also go to class each week to get more info. What's even better is that people at WFG are caring and friendly. They're not pushy. That being said, every company has good agents; I hope you'll be able to find them, too.

I decided to join the financial business world and write this book because I've gained so much knowledge from WFG. I've consolidated my portfolio, and my investments are doing so much better than before.

Step 5: Build Passive (Residual) Income. Depending on your age, you need to look at the possibility of creating residual income. It isn't just for your financial independence but also to keep your brain working. There are many different types of residual income:

1. Rental properties: Buying properties to flip or to rent.

2. Dividend-paying stock: Warren Buffett allows his money to work for him. He buys a share of a stock that pays dividends, and each month or quarter, he gets paid. The more stocks you buy, the

larger that residual income becomes—to the point where Buffett earns roughly $62 million a year on dividend payments.

3. Running a small business part-time or full-time.

4. Running an online store.

5. Etc.

I've been an independent IT consultant and employee all my 40 years in the workforce. I heard about residual income but never really looked into it much. Then, after I semi-retired, I was invited to a meeting. I found it very interesting. I hope you consider it as a way to get a better handle on your financial situation. It gives me great pleasure to see you flourish.

Step 6: Focus on the Three Ds.

1. **Diversify:** I'm sure you've heard about not putting all your eggs in one basket. So, when you consolidate your assets, you need to check them by category. For example, if you have 80% of your assets in real estate, you should use your money to buy something else. Even if you love real estate, you don't want to be caught in a down market and lose everything.

2. **Dollar Cost Averaging:** It's better to buy a little bit of a stock, mutual fund, or segregated fund each month. When the market is up, you end up buying less, but you buy more when the market is down, so it averages out.

3. Cultivate **Discipline:** You need to be consistent in your saving efforts and not wait until you're in your late 50's to start saving. It's important to save consistently now and let your money do the work for you over time.

Step 7: Help Others. I help my family members, but I always felt I wasn't good enough to help others. I thought there were people better than me who provided support for them. But now, I've changed my mindset. If a grade six student can help someone in grade five or below, and university students can help high school students, I can help you. You don't need to wait until you're perfect before you start helping. If you wait until you've learned everything before you do anything, the day that you can do something will never come.

There are many areas where you can help: Volunteer at a non-profit organization, hospital, school, political party, church, etc. I volunteer to help CPAs in the financial literacy area. I do presentations and help construct personal financial strategies for attendees. I'm also an agent in World Financial Group. Since I've done many personal financial strategies, I can share what I've learned, so you achieve a better retirement.

You can also take part in other part-time or full-time businesses. It's never too late to do a business part-time or full-time. The sooner you start, the better it is. You just need to begin small and get a handle on how to become successful. It took Elon Musk three failed businesses before he got his fourth chance in North America. He's now the second richest man alive.

You can do it as well. You may be successful on a smaller scale, but it never hurts to give it a try. It will also keep you learning and your brain active.

Step 8: Take Time to Enjoy Life. Life isn't always about work. Take the time to relax and enjoy life with your family. We only live once, so why not take advantage of eating, travel, explore, relax, and have some fun? But because everyone has a different way of enjoying, I'll leave this section for you to discover.

Go to AMoneyMasterMillionaire.com for the following bonuses:

Retirement Ready Assessment

Five Estate Planning Must-Haves

Money Master Millionaire in the Making

Cashflow 101 Workbook .

30-Minute Personal Consultation Session

www.ingramcontent.com/pod-product-compliance
Lightning Source LLC
Chambersburg PA
CBHW071209200326
41519CB00018B/5435